A Handbook
of
Christian Doctrine

A Handbook
of
Christian Doctrine

by
Charles E. Brown

a subsidiary of Church of God Ministries, Inc.
ANDERSON, INDIANA

Coordinator of Communications and Publishing
Church of God Ministries, Inc.
PO Box 2420
Anderson, IN 46018-2420
800-848-2464
www.chog.org

To purchase additional copies of this book, to inquire about distribution and for all other sales-related matters, please contact:

Warner Press, Inc.
PO Box 2499
Anderson, IN 46018-9988
877-346-3974
www.warnerpress.com

Cover design by Mary Jaracz
Indexes by Joseph D. Allison

ISBN-13: 978-1-59317-141-1
ISBN-10: 1-59317-141-2

Printed in Canada.
06 07 08 09 10 / TC / 10 9 8 7 6 5 4 3 2 1

PUBLISHER'S PREFACE

Charles Ewing Brown (1883–1971) began his public ministry as a boy preacher traveling with his father, an evangelist from eastern Kentucky named Willis M. Brown. Their itinerant work cut short Charles's formal education, yet the Browns' ministry required a good working knowledge of Scripture, Christian doctrine, and church history.

In the late 1800s, doctrinal debates were an effective way for evangelists to gather an audience, and the traveling Browns often did this. They debated Christian Scientists, Jehovah's Witnesses, and denominational leaders of every stripe. Charles read voraciously to prepare for these debates. As a result, he became a capable, articulate evangelist of the Holiness Movement. He and his father were allied with a Holiness group known as the Church of God reformation movement, which proclaimed that all God's people can live in personal holiness and visible unity with other Christians.

Even after Charles became pastor of a large Church of God congregation in Detroit, he pursued a life of diligent scholarship. He wrote several books and tracts, including one based on the doctrinal debates of his early days (*Christian Science Unmasked*, 1919). His preaching and writing caught the attention of national Church of God leaders, who named him editor in chief of their weekly magazine, the *Gospel Trumpet*. Charles served in that post from 1930 to 1951. He wrote hundreds of articles and more than a dozen books on doctrine and church history. His two best-known books, *The Meaning of Salvation* (1944) and *The Meaning of Sanctification* (1945), are still in print.

Despite his lack of formal theological education, Brown's self-disciplined mastery of these subjects brought him an honorary doctor of divinity degree from Anderson College (now Anderson University). He became associate professor of church history there, which enabled him to continue his prolific study and writing.

Though not as well known as his other books, this volume has a significant place in Brown's legacy to the church. Originally published in 1957 under the title *We Preach Christ*, it is a concise, Christ-centered introduction to theology. So it seems fitting to use his original subtitle as the title of this reissued book: *A Handbook of Christian Doctrine.*

Dr. Brown's thesis is that Jesus Christ is the lens through which all of God's truth comes into clearest focus. Books of systematic theology commonly use the didactic categories of Greek philosophy to guide our exploration of Christian theology; however, Brown believes our only reliable guide to eternal matters is the Bible. The Christian faith is rationally coherent; yet Brown reminds us that reason has its limits, and the deepest knowledge of theology comes only through a personal relationship with God.

The church owes a great debt to Dr. Brown. It can only be repaid by the reverent study of God's Word and the faithful embodiment of God's truth in our daily lives.

CONTENTS

PART TWO

THE WORK OF CHRIST AS PRIEST

PART THREE

THE WORK OF CHRIST AS KING

INTRODUCTION

Theology is the systematization and interpretation of the teachings of the divine revelation. Some people object to this type of study on the ground that the revelation is not systematically presented in the Bible. This objection could be brought against each of the natural sciences which all proceed along the same lines. Scholars collect and systematize the facts of their subject and then seek to interpret them.

Take geology for example. Probably no geologist knows the natural surface of the earth as well as primitive man does. But the savage sees only the surface while the geologist collates all the facts he can gather over the whole earth; then comparing and interpreting these facts, he develops theories which finally crystallize into the science of geology. He knows that this science is essentially true because he can make use of it to find the oil, the coal, the iron, and the various treasures of the earth.

The Bible is like the earth. The earth appears so simple that men trod upon it for ages without sensing any mystery, without asking any relevant questions. It seemed simple; nevertheless, it contained in itself the very sum and substance of all science, such as physics, chemistry, metallurgy, electricity, radiology, and the like. The Bible seems just as simple as the earth—and it is. But it has within it vast hidden treasures of truth which give scope for the exercise of more than all the intellectual powers of the greatest human genius. Primitive man could find upon the generous bosom of Mother Earth all the food necessary for his existence at a time when he was in complete ignorance that the earth was a scientific laboratory of the utmost complexity.

Did man do wrong, then, in developing science? No. Almost

the earliest of God's commands to him was to "subdue" the earth (Gen. 1:28). And man subdues the earth as much by science as by labor. Moreover, by science alone is it possible for him to find as much food as is necessary in this age when he has succeeded so well in replenishing the earth with a population of teeming millions. In fact, it can be truthfully said that the real cause of hunger in non-Christian lands is the lack of science which knows how to make food as abundant as in the countries trained in science. The study of science has not only made food more abundant, but it has also multiplied all other comforts of life. Better than all this, it has nurtured the development of man.

Likewise we believe the systematic study of the Bible will provide food for the soul and facilitate the development of the spiritual side of man's life.

If the Bible is a revelation from God why is it so complex and mystifying? Let us turn again to our use of the earth as a parable. The earth is the creation of God, yet it is the most confusing and mysterious enigma possible to imagine. As we have said, all the sciences are hidden in it, clear up to the last book and the last experiment.

Evidently the Eternal Teacher intends to keep man learning in His school of nature as long as time endures. And perhaps our Father never intends for us to graduate from the school of Christ.

Again there is another reason for the confused appearance of the earth to a young learner, though not to a scientist. The earth was made primarily for use and secondarily for study; for all mankind must see it, but only a few gifted persons have the duty of studying it. For example, a typewriter or watch is not easy to understand for an ignorant person. Why did not the inventors of these machines make them easy to study? Because they did not make them primarily for study but for use. Nevertheless certain persons must study typewriters and watches and many other kinds of machinery in order to learn how to repair them, to duplicate them, to use them successfully, and to improve them. So it is with the Bible. Its use is more important than its systematic study—considered merely as an end in itself—but its systematic study greatly facilitates its use and advantage to the general welfare of the soul.

The science of geology never produced a barrel of oil or a ton of coal, but it has taught men how to bring forth millions of barrels of oil and mountains of coal from the formerly hidden and unknown resources of the earth. Likewise a true theology will facilitate the acquisition of the treasures of the Word of God. This fact lays upon the writer the burden of preparing this book, and it also lays upon the conscience of the reader the solemn duty of bestowing real labor upon its study —no less, in fact, than he would give to the study of a secular science.

The Bible is the revelation of God. Theology is the fruit of the work which men have done upon the Bible, just as a vegetable garden is the result of man's work upon the naked earth. The first preaching was for immediate use among unlearned and common men. Theology as a discipline was of slow growth, and finally came to definite shape in combination with the thought forms of Greek philosophy. This fact has long been used as a discouragement to the study of theology altogether. That Greek philosophy strongly influenced ancient theology should not be considered as a curse upon all theology, but rather as a clear challenge to all theologians to avoid the tares among the wheat. For example, most works on systematic theology begin with a discussion of God which consists of a combination of ideas of God drawn from the Greek philosophers as far back as the fifth century before Christ combined with scriptural ideas of God drawn from the Bible. This traditional theology has become so acclimated in the Christian tradition that we do not feel disposed to discuss it critically within this brief space. Suffice it to state our belief that all we can actually know about God is what is revealed to us in Christ, the revealer of God. We believe in the God of the traditional theology, but we believe that certain shades of meaning which have crept in from philosophy will tend to gain a more correct perspective if we view them entirely from the viewpoint of the revelation of God in Christ.

We believe we have gained a new insight into Christian doctrine when we see it, not as a miscellaneous bundle of theories about many debatable subjects, but rather as an organic body of truth rooted in the person of Jesus Christ. The doctrine of Christ grows out of the nature of Christ. It is a description of the character and habits (work) of Christ. It tells who he is, what he does, and why and how he does it. Viewed in this way it becomes apparent that whoever loves Christ must love his doctrine, for in the doctrine of Christ is comprised all that we know, or can know about his person and work.

Christ is God. "In the beginning was the Word, and the Word was with God, and the Word was God" (John 1:1). (Theology.)

Christ is creator. "All things were made by him; and without him was not anything made that was made" (1:3). (Works of God.)

Christ is rejected of men. "He is despised and rejected of men" (Isa. 53:3). (Doctrine of sin.)

Christ is the atonement for sin. "And he is the propitiation for our sins" (I John 2:2). (Soteriology.)

Christ is the redeemer. "He shall save his people from their sins" (Matt. 1:21).

Christ is the sanctifier. "Jesus also, that he might sanctify the people with his own blood suffered . . ." (Heb. 13:12).

Christ is head of the church. ". . . even as Christ is the head of the church" (Eph. 5:23). (Ecclesiology.)

Christ is the resurrection. "I am the resurrection and the life" (John 11:25). (Eschatology.)

Christ is judge of all men. "For we must all appear before the judgment seat of Christ" (II Cor. 5:10).

Before closing the introduction the reader should be apprised that this is a handbook. Anything like a fair treatment of

Christian doctrine must fill a large space. Hodge's *Theology* comprises three massive volumes, each containing apparently as much material as the whole Bible. Our work must be sharply abbreviated. Now in condensing the treatment of a subject two courses are possible: One may squeeze all the material into small space. In a work of this kind that would mean the production of little more than a catalogue of all the subjects demanding attention in a complete discussion of the theme. Such a book could but be insufferably dry. Another method would be to cut out large areas of discussion and present only what seems most relevant to the needs of the student in the beginning of such studies. This is the method chosen here, and it is not without distinguished precedent, being in fact the very method followed by such popular religious writers as C. S. Lewis, and others.

As previously stated, ancient theology arose when the primitive preaching of the church was accepted by men with Greek education and began to be interpreted in terms of Greek thought. Sometimes this philosophic influence was so strong as to weaken the truth of the Christian message. That truth is found in the saying of Jesus Christ: "All things are delivered unto me of my Father: and no man knoweth the Son, but the Father; neither knoweth any man the Father, save the Son, and he to whomsoever the Son will reveal him" (Matt. 11:27).

From this we draw the plain truth that there is no clear revelation of God except in Jesus Christ.

PART ONE

THE WORK OF CHRIST AS PROPHET

INTRODUCTION: PROPHET AND PROPHECY

From the days of ancient Christianity theologians have divided the work of Christ into three parts, those of Prophet, Priest, and King. We shall follow that plan in the division of our work. These terms need exposition.

Few words are more misunderstood among Christians of our day than "prophet" and "prophecy." A prophet is usually considered solely as one who predicts—often as little better than a fortuneteller. Actually the truth is far different. In the Old Testament the term for prophet is a Hebrew word which is derived from a root which means "to bubble up," as a spring in the desert. The word therefore signifies a man in whose soul the word of God bubbles up. In New Testament Greek the prophet is a man who speaks for another, an ambassador. Combining these we get the idea of a man of God in whose heart the word of God is bubbling up and who is sent of God as an ambassador.

The large element of prediction in the prophets may be accounted for by the fact that the burden of Old Testament prophecy was concerned with the Christ who should come to Israel. "The testimony of Jesus is the spirit of prophecy" (Rev. 19:10). However, since the testimony of Jesus in New Testament prophecy is concerned with the Christ who has already come, there is very little of the predictive element in New Testament prophecy. We speak of the Christ who has come and is now present and alive in his church. The work of a prophet in the New Testament age is that of a preacher and teacher.

Moses said, "The Lord thy God will raise up unto thee a Prophet from the midst of thee, of thy brethren, like unto me; unto him ye shall hearken" (Deut. 18:15). Jesus Christ was that prophet. See Acts 3:22-24.

In the following section we study Christ's work as teacher in revealing God and God's work. In the section on Christ as priest we will study the necessity and nature of Christ's work in atoning for sin and reconciling men to God. Under the caption of Christ as King we will study Christ's work of ruling the kingdom of God and bringing an end to the present world.

Chapter I

CHRIST, THE REVEALER OF GOD

Many years ago in a tiny restaurant in Yokohama, Japan, an old Japanese told me a touching story of his youth as an enslaved laborer on a Japanese pearl-fishing boat off the coast of Australia. There his heart hungered for God with such an aching that he was tempted to kill himself. As he stood on the deck of his vessel under the faraway stars pondering whether to end it all by one desperate leap into the purple waters, a cry of agony was wrung from his soul, a prayer to the eternal mystery that seemed hidden beyond the solemn face of the night.

So it has ever been with men. They have always believed that beyond time and space and the brooding silence of nature there stands an answer to their most tormenting question. "Canst thou by searching find out God?" (Job 11:7). For generations orthodox theologians have discussed this question.

THE NECESSITY OF A DIVINE REVELATION

At the very time when modern scientific materialism has done its utmost to convince men that they are simply animals, and no more, a mass of evidence has accumulated to indicate that, though men are indeed animals, they are *much more* than animals. And it is in the nature of man which is much more than animal that there lies the longing and the need for the revelation of God—a longing deep as the heart of man and as old as humanity itself.

Man Is More than Animal

As mere animals men would be satisfied with what nature supplies. Scientific inquiry indicates that the animals are content with the provisions of nature, if these are only fairly adequate. But with men the case is far different. Not only does the supply of natural wants fail to satisfy them; such a supply seems to increase their discontent. Here is a problem for science. In America food is so abundant that an estimated 45 per cent of the people are overfed, and, more or less, striving to reduce weight. Vast surpluses of food constitute one of our gravest political problems. Does this fact tend to increase our happiness? Far from it. It is almost an axiom that while good feeding and care tend to make cows content, such provision commonly proves otherwise with men. They are never really happy till they find God. Caged and well-fed animals are usually quite content, but there is no misery greater than that of caged and well-fed men, because men are more than animals.

In the eighteenth century Malthus started speculation which developed into the doctrine of evolution by propounding the theory that the increase of population always tends to outrun the food supply. If man were not more than animal this would be so, but by the use of science far outreaching the abilities of any mere animal, man has developed such vast possibilities of practically unlimited food supplies that the problem is fairly well solved for scientifically progressive communities, as the example of America tends to show, though America has not even begun to develop the newly discovered possibilities. Yet the utopia of man's contentment is further removed than ever, because he has spiritual needs which science cannot supply.

Man's Spiritual Nature Unsatisfied

So vast are the resources of nature and of science that men today might be living in an earthly paradise if they were no more than animals. But because they are more than animals, and because the animal-plus quality of their nature is unsatisfied, they are more miserable than ever before in history. Furthermore, the animal-plus (spiritual) quality of man's nature is so perverted, even in his relations with his fellows, that crime and war, the fruits of this perversion, constantly load him with increasing misery.

For example, every child born into the citizenship of the United States is immediately burdened with his share of the national debt in an amount which would have paid his way through college at the time when the debt was incurred. Add to this the cost of crime, and his burden is thereby immensely increased. Thus science and social reform have failed to bring us to utopia. We are more than animals, and our animal-plus nature is out of adjustment with humanity—and with God.

Materialists boast of evolution and the redemption of man to be wrought by science, yet after approximately one short century of living under the belief in evolution, we are pained by the agony of a universal cold war and horrified by the fear of ever more menacing bombs. This conscious agonizing misery of man is due to a flaw in that part of his being which is more than animal—a flaw which causes a fundamental maladjustment with his brothers. And he is out of harmony with his brothers primarily because he is not right with God. The very fact that he has hell upon earth instead of his theoretically possible paradise is proof of his need of a revelation—an unveiling of God.

It may be objected that we have proved too much, that we have not only proved that we need a revelation, but also that we do not have a revelation—at least not one sufficient to our need. The reply is that we seek to prove man's need of a revelation. This in nowise proves that man does not have such a revelation. Man is free, and he might have a revelation without using it. Failure to use the revelation does not decrease his need of it, but such a fact ought to increase the zeal of Christians in spreading the knowledge of that revelation.

God Has Revealed Himself

Today, the stream of thought follows channels different from those of the old theological discussions. A hundred years ago men battled hard over the question of God's existence. Today the majority believe in the existence of God, but without passion or conviction, and the minority deny the existence of God, but with indifferent toleration. Evidence which satisfies us that man needs a revelation, will inferentially prove both its possibility and probability; for if God is God, he knows of man's need and more than probably will supply it.

The Bible Reveals God

Our generation is not given to theory. We do not argue about what ought to be, but what is. In fact we have a body of literature called the Bible which boldly professes to be a supernatural revelation from God. Arguments about that book have filled polemic literature for generations. These arguments are a battle of giants; they cover questions of history, criticism, philosophy, logic, and science. They are about God and the Bible; for if there is no God, then no evidence can uphold the Bible. On the other hand if the Bible is not authoritative, there is such an all-pervading uncertainty about the kind of God— if any—we have left, that the very foundations of human society are shaken to their depths.

Many think that spiritual Christians have no duty to engage in this discussion. It is even wrong to do so, because the Bible and Christianity need no defense—only the witness of men and women of fine character. For years I have pondered these things, and I believe that, though sin is the strongest root of unbelief—sin will dull the vision of an intentionally honest man—nevertheless, honest intellectual doubt may injure the moral life of sincere people even though they have a high purpose to be intellectually honest. For this reason it is a laudable work to clear away the impediments to faith, to destroy the intellectual and philosophical arguments which blind the minds of honest men.

However, the limitations of this book are such that we cannot enter this controversy here. We dare no more than point out that persons concerned have ample room for research in this field. The most powerful of all arguments is so simple that a child can understand it. It was made by the blind man healed by Christ: "One thing I know, that, whereas I was blind, now I see" (John 9:25). This is the argument: If the Bible is accepted as a revelation, it works like one. It makes a thief honest, a liar truthful, a drunkard sober; it gives a sad man a joyful hope of heaven.

Simplicity and Mystery of the Bible

The Bible is probably the greatest paradox in human life, at once so simple and so complex, so naive and so deep in mystery. Once I knew a very pious but illiterate man who frankly and without bluster admitted that he was master of the whole New Testament. Any New Testament scholar, able to read the book fluently in Greek and thoroughly grounded in all branches of New Testament scholarship—any such man who would make such a profession would be promptly branded as insane. I now think that the illiterate brother was actually correct in his claims, for he had that which is hidden "from the wise and prudent, and . . . revealed . . . unto babes" (Matt. 11:25). Nevertheless, it remains true that for "the wise and prudent" the Bible still remains the most difficult book in the world. Why did God permit a revelation of himself to be encumbered with a thousand incomprehensible mysteries?

Humility does not deny us an answer here, for the answer is simple. Just as the inventors of watches and clocks and household machinery did not make the machines for study but for use—just as the earth is made for use—so the Bible is made for use.

But somebody must study the machinery, the earth, and the Bible. And if in study one finds mysteries that baffle him, questions that he cannot answer, he should not be a fool and throw away a useful article on this account.

THE RELATION OF REASON AND FAITH

Almost all traditional theology is vitiated by a false distinction between faith and reason, setting them in opposition.

This confusion of thought rises out of the many meanings of the word "faith." In the English language every word has from five to hundreds of meanings—often through the use of metaphor. Faith means trust in a person, acceptance of a person's statements as facts, acceptance of a set of statements and opinions as truth. In the Bible, often it signifies a spiritual sensitivity or awareness of the reality of eternal truths and relations, rising to an awareness of God and an actual knowledge of him as a divine person. This spiritual sensitivity is often compared to the five physical senses: smell, taste, touch, hearing, and sight. All of these senses are used to describe spiritual experience: ". . . his smell as Lebanon" (Hos. 14: 6). "Taste and see that the Lord is good" (Ps. 34: 8). "Lo, this hath touched thy lips; . . . thy sin is purged" (Isa. 6: 7). "He that is of God heareth God's words" (John 8: 47). "Blessed are the pure in heart: for they shall see God" (Matt. 5: 8). This beatitude makes clear that the capacity for spiritual vision is conditioned by the moral state of the heart.

Contrast Faith and Physical Senses

The foregoing texts prove that the powers of the soul to apprehend spiritual phenomena are exactly paired with the physical senses which observe physical phenomena. But inasmuch as sight is the most powerful of all the senses, it may safely be used as a symbol of all the spiritual capacities of the soul to become aware of spiritual realities, including personal knowledge of God. In the Bible this sensitivity is called faith.

Thus we see that the contrast is never one between faith and reason, but between faith and the bodily senses—between faith and the body of knowledge based only on the physical senses. When the bodily senses bring a report that the house is on fire, reason gives a judgment ordering retreat, and thus the man is saved from burning. In the case of a martyr the spiritual senses bring a report that the only way of escape involves a denial of Christ (a fact that the physical senses cannot grasp). Here the reason gives the judgment of conscience—this escape will be sinful—and it also gives the decision of the will: No. Thus it was the reason which gave the judgment in each case. In one case the judgment was built on the report of the physical senses. In the other case the reason gave a judgment built upon the report of the spiritual senses (the vision of faith) and decided martyrdom preferable to recanting. "No man can say that Jesus is Lord, but by the Holy Ghost" (I Cor. 12:3).

Reason Is Intellect at Work

Reason is not a "faculty" of the mind, as was formerly thought. Reason is simply intellectual activity. The powers of the mind are simply different ways in which the mind acts. When we speak of a boy running, riding, and swimming, we do not mention different faculties of the boy's being, but different activities of his one body. So intellect, emotion, and will are not three different faculties of the mind, but are simply the mind thinking, feeling, and willing. Reason, then, is not a faculty of the mind, but an activity of the mind or soul, as observing, comparing, judging. If this observing, comparing, judging, is done on the basis of reports from the spiritual world brought by the "senses" we call faith, the judgment will doubtless be quite different from a judgment founded upon a report from the physical senses, but whatever the judgment it can never be anything but a judgment of the reason. Thus we see there never can be a conflict between faith and reason, for acts of faith, such as that of enduring martyrdom, are based upon the exercise of reason as truly as is the rationalistic atheist's denial of the existence of God.

One may well be amazed at the different patterns of behavior which the reason follows. In one case we have the study of art and the canons of taste by which an art critic judges a work of art; then we have the kinds of thinking normal for an engineer, a novelist, a poet, a musician, a biologist, a psychologist, a salesman, or an attorney pleading before a court. In each of these cases the practical exigencies of his daily work create in his mind such widely different apperceptions and prejudices and such wholly different approaches to the truth, that one might fairly call each man's mind by a different name.

Reason Is "Heart" of Religious Man

Different also is the habit of thought built up in the mind of a religious man. In popular language, and also in the language of the Bible, this whole world of thought fashioned in the mind of a religious man is called the "heart." Remember that the reasoning power of an artist, such as a poet, novelist, or musician, is also called by the same name. And if we are discussing problems of modern thought and criticism, we must remember that the "heart" of the artist and man of religion is nothing other than the reason of the soul—reason trained to make a special response, perhaps, but reason, nonetheless. Thus there never can arise a conflict between reason and faith, any more than between reason and sight or reason and hearing. And it is absurd to ask a man to deny the verdict of his reason in favor of a different opinion, for if he should deny the verdict of reason he would have nothing to do it with except the power of reason itself. And if he does change, on the basis of fresh evidence furnished, perhaps, by the eye of faith, it is still his reason which makes the new verdict.

This settles the question of rational or irrational theology. There is no such thing possible as irrational theology. Here one must remember that there is a so-called rationalistic theology which is thoroughly skeptical. However, it is not one whit more rational than the theology of Irenaeus or Augustine. It is simply based upon the reports of the physical senses as such while its eyes are stubbornly blinded to the reports of the organs of the spirit which sense the realities of eternity.

THE QUESTION OF CERTITUDE

"How shall I know that I shall inherit it?" Abraham asked God concerning the land of Canaan. It is one of the most agonizing questions of this age of scientific materialism. From ancient times recurring generations of thinkers have stressed universal skepticism and harped on man's inability really to find truth in any field. These skeptics make a practice of pointing to the endless conflict in the theories and opinions of men. They assert that the critics dispute about all matters of opinion in every field of human work. These arguments have upset many young thinkers in the past.

Man Can Know

The answer to all this is that at least in certain areas of science men have given positive proof that the mind of man can apprehend reality correctly and reason wisely on its laws. Proof of this is found in the successful work of science in every field of industrial engineering. Especially is this success notable in the building of the atom bomb. In these fields the most raucous skeptic cannot deny that men have learned the truth about nature and have reasoned correctly concerning the application of natural laws. Here the skeptic is overwhelmed with proof of the clearest kind and his carping made ridiculous.

These facts do not prove that man can ever find the truth in the fields of philosophy and religion, but they break the negative bar of skepticism regarding the power of the human reason to know the truth about a given phase of life when the basic facts are supplied in sufficient amount and man reasons about them correctly. When we turn to the quarry of religious truth—the Bible—we learn definitely: "Ye shall know the truth, and the truth shall make you free."

Pragmatic Test of Truth Insufficient

Science tests theories by the so-called pragmatic test: "Do they work?" The Bible knows such a test: "By their fruits shall ye know them." When a scientist tells you he knows how to make a talking machine, you must believe him when his machine actually talks. Undoubtedly the pragmatic test stands approved in modern science.

Nevertheless, the pragmatic test does not stand so high in religious and philosophical discussion. And I think the reason must be that in the latter fields the test is so much harder to apply. For example, it would be easy to say that a pragmatic test of the truth of a religion would be the success of that religion in winning converts. This seems fair on the surface, but results are surprising. There is at this writing a certain religious leader in America who claims to be God Almighty. This man has actually made 500,000 converts in the last twenty years and claims forty times that number. But does this success make him God?

By the test of success Protestantism would be true in America and Romanism in Europe, whereas Islam would be truer than either of them, and paganism would be truer than Islam. And if communism, as I believe, should be called a religion, who would admit that its success proved its truth? If the free sale of opium were legalized in America, who will believe that its use would not win out over the services of the scientific physicians? Herein is indicated one of the reasons why the pragmatic test is not more successful in religion. It is too subjective. A man with a terrible and painful disease might derive more relief and enjoyment from the use of opium than from the services of the best physician, even though the opium would kill him in the end and the physician might be able to cure him.

If it were possible, however, to set up a just and correct pragmatic test, it would be found to reveal the truth in any doctrine. Belief in, and practice of, a true doctrine will make an individual better morally, happier emotionally, and better adjusted—relatively speaking—socially. A congregation that knows and practices the truth will foster moral idealism and tend to make the Christian way of life seem glorious. The members will nurture a warm Christian fellowship which promotes spirituality within the congregation and spreads it abroad. Such is the fruit of the divine revelation.

Christ Is the Revelation

Christ said, "He that hath seen me hath seen the Father." This of course means that Christ was the very revelation of

God. In him "God was manifest in the flesh (I Tim. 3:16). At the height of Old Testament prophecy the people were exhorted, "Behold your God" (Isa. 40:9), but in the supreme tragedy of the crucifixion, the cry was "Behold the Man!" (John 19:5). In Christ "are hid all the treasures of wisdom and knowledge." No revelation is genuine which is not derived from him. There can be no revelation outside of him. All speculation is vain. Christian theology arose when the simple preaching of the apostolic church met the philosophy of Greece. In shaping theology into an academic discipline, the earliest theologians tended to introduce philosophical concepts inharmonious with the unveiling of God in Christ. For example, the Greek philosophers taught that God could not love, for to love is to desire, and to desire is to suffer. God, they said, cannot desire anything. He is supremely self-sufficient. He cannot love, therefore. All men love him, in the sense that they desire his benefits, but he does not love anybody, for he needs nothing. Neither can he suffer.

But Jesus taught: "No man knoweth the Son, but the Father; neither knoweth any man the Father, save the Son, and he to whomsoever the Son will reveal him" (Matt. 11:27). Jesus contradicted Greek philosophy by teaching: "God so loved the world, that he gave his only begotten Son . . . " (John 3:16). And he taught that God suffered in Christ.

The meaning of all this is that we must cut loose from all the philosophical prejudices of ancient theology, and commit ourselves to that only which is to be known about God through the revelation of Christ. He says: "I am . . . the truth" (John 14:6). He is the mediator between God and man. Not only the last book of the Bible, but the entire Bible from Genesis to Revelation is the revelation of Jesus Christ (Rev. 1:1).

ASPECTS OF REVELATION

Although a few theologians deny it, the great majority believe that there are two forms or stages of the work of revelation, variously called general and special or natural and supernatural. We agree that there exists both a natural and supernatural revelation of God.

How Natural and Supernatural Differ

In order to clarify this distinction let us first explore the difference between the natural and the supernatural. Research will establish that the phenomenon of consciousness is so unique in the world of man's knowledge that practically every term used to describe it is drawn from the physical world and attributed to our inner world of thought by a metaphorical extension of meaning. Thus "apprehension" is the putting forth of the hand to take anything; "understand" is literally to stand under; "comprehension" is the taking of things together in a handful, and so forth. Thus, when we pass from the unselfconscious world of nature to the self-conscious world of living persons we pass into a new order of life only describable by figures of speech. It is commonly regarded that the animals lack self-consciousness, at least in the sense and degree known by man.

Self-consciousness is the dividing line between the lower forms of animal consciousness and the nobler personality of man. Mr. Jones owns an automatic machine which does his will in manufacturing goods which he values. Although this machine has built into it a prearranged pattern of intelligence, and its products are therefore the products of intelligent thought nevertheless the nature of these products must continue to be uniform until and unless the owner moves a setting screw which causes the machine to turn out a different pattern.

The Meaning of Miracle

This is a parable of the meaning of miracle. Miracle is always something which occurs in the realm of the divine self-consciousness. The rationalistic objection that a miracle would be an unworthy interference by God with his settled order of nature is puerile. Such manipulation of the divinely constituted order of nature is not a mark of God's weakness and ignorance, but of his wisdom and power. In the divine governance of the world, when God is dealing with millions of free persons, it is a mark of wisdom that he retains the power to create such changes in the world processes as are necessary to make a wise response to the changing needs of men. Weak mortal man has marvelous power to manipulate these natural processes, as the growth of scientific industrialism proves. To deny equal and even greater power to the omniscient and omnipotent God is to degrade him below man.

When two men talk to each other they function in the realm of human self-consciousness, or personality. All prayer and real worship, all true communion with God, all answers to prayer (yes, and all specific denials of requests which reach God as real prayer)—all these take place in the realm of the supernatural. These all belong to the realm of divine self-consciousness wherein we commune with God as a person. All this is miraculous, the prayer denied fully as much as the prayer granted. For the miracle lies in getting a human petition before the throne of God as a real prayer, and not as a murmur in the ceaseless roar of human suffering and selfish longings.

> I have felt
> A presence that disturbs me with the joy
> Of elevated thoughts; a sense sublime
> Of something far more deeply interfused,
> Whose dwelling is the light of setting suns,
> And the round ocean and the living air,
> And the blue sky, and in the mind of man.
> —Wordsworth,
> in "Lines on Tintern Abbey"

God Revealed in Nature

No Christian is permitted to deny that God makes a revelation of himself in nature, for the fact lies upon the face of Scripture in numerous positive assertions: "The heavens declare the glory of God; and the firmament showeth his handiwork. Day unto day uttereth speech, and night unto night showeth knowledge" (Ps. 19:1). "When I consider thy heavens, the work of thy fingers, the moon and the stars which thou hast ordained" (8:2). "Because that which may be known of God is manifest in them; for God hath showed it to them. For the invisible things of him from the creation of the world are clearly seen, being understood by the things that are made, even his eternal power and Godhead; so that they are without excuse" (Rom. 1:19-20).

This subject of natural revelation of God is a favorite theme of Paul's. At Lystra he taught the pagans that God "left not himself without witness, in that he did good, and gave us rain from heaven, and fruitful seasons, filling our hearts with food and gladness" (Acts 14:17).

Paul even went beyond physical nature and taught that there is a secret law of God inscribed on the hearts of all men. "For when the Gentiles, which have not the law, do by nature the things contained in the law, these, having not the law, are a law unto themselves: which show the work of the law written in their hearts, their conscience also bearing witness, and their thoughts the meanwhile accusing or else excusing one another. . . . Therefore if the uncircumcision keep the righteousness of the law, shall not his uncircumcision be counted for circumcision?" (Rom. 2:14-15, 26).

Peter testifies to the same truth: "Of a truth I perceive that God is no respecter of persons: but in every nation he that feareth him, and worketh righteousness, is accepted with him" (Acts 10:34-35). This is possible because all men are "his offspring" (17:28). All men have the capacity to feel after him, and find him" (vs. 27).

THE SUPERNATURAL REVELATION

This is the revelation mentioned by the writer of the Epistle to the Hebrews: "God, who at sundry times and in divers manners spake in time past unto the fathers by the prophets, hath in these last days spoken unto us by his Son" (1:1). It is through this Son that all the revelation, both natural and supernatural, was made. "Of which salvation the prophets have inquired and searched diligently, who prophesied of the grace that should come unto you: searching what, or what manner of time the Spirit of Christ which was in them did signify, when it testified beforehand the sufferings of Christ, and the glory that should follow" (I Pet. 1:10-11). These Scripture passages tell us that the messages of the prophets in the Old Testament came as part of the work of Christ as revealer of God, and if the supernatural revelation came from Christ, no less so did the natural revelation which was governed by Christ in the creation of the world. See John 1:3.

Christ is the supreme Master, or Teacher: "One is your Master even Christ" (Matt. 23:8). He drowns out the great voices of the past with his "But I say unto you" (5:22). It is the Holy Spirit who conveys the messages of revelation to the world: "I have yet many things to say unto you, but ye cannot bear them now. Howbeit when he, the Spirit of truth, is come, he will guide you into all truth: for he shall not speak of himself. . . . He shall glorify me; for he shall receive of mine, and shall show it unto you" (John 16:12-14). It is the Holy Spirit whose divine utterances make up the body of Scripture: "All scripture is given by inspiration of God, and is profitable" (II Tim. 3:16). However, the message of the Holy Spirit is not primarily concerned with the marvels of land and sea and stories of ancient peoples. Its primary concern is Christ and his salvation. The Holy Spirit "shall testify of me" (John 15:26). "Great is the mystery of godliness: God was manifest in the flesh" (I Tim. 3:16). This is the "mystery of God" in Christ.

Browning sings of faith:

> *If I stoop*
> *Into a dark tremendous sea of cloud*
> *It is but for a time; I press God's lamp*
> *Close to my breast; its splendor soon or late*
> *Will pierce the gloom: I shall emerge one day.*

Christ is "the Word" (John 1:1). And "he that hath seen me hath seen the Father" (14:9). Christ completes the revelation of God in the Old Testament, for he came not "to destroy, but to fulfill" (Matt. 5:17). Christ's revelation is "from faith to faith." That is, it is given through believers to men willing to believe. Sin destroys faith and makes the acceptance of the revelation slow and difficult, for "the natural man receiveth not the things of the Spirit of God: for they are foolishness unto him: neither can he know them, because they are spiritually discerned" (I Cor. 2:14). "There is a spirit in man: and the inspiration of the Almighty giveth them understanding" (Job 32:8). "But he that doeth truth cometh to the light" (John 3:21). That light is Christ who is "the true Light, which lighteth every man that cometh into the world" (1:9). One must be of the truth to hear his voice (18:37). And one must will to do His will in order to know of the doctrine (7:17), for the Holy Spirit is the Spirit of truth (16:13). All unbelievers are blinded by the god of this world: "In whom the god of this world hath blinded the minds of them which believe not, lest the light of the glorious gospel of Christ, who is the image of God, should shine unto them" (II Cor. 4:4). This is "the light of the knowledge of the glory of God in the face of Jesus Christ" (vs. 6).

We have used these Scripture verses to show that standing behind all the record of the revelation in the Bible and all the means of revelation in nature is the one Revealer of God, our Lord Jesus Christ. It was he who spake through the prophets and writers of the Old Testament, and it was his face dimly discerned in nature from ancient days that brought the thought of God into the minds of men. He is the mirror of God. Therefore, "we all, with open face beholding as in a glass the glory of the Lord, are changed into the same image, from glory to glory" (II Cor. 3:18). That expresses the purpose of the revelation: not to satisfy all our curiosity, or answer all our questions, but to change us into His image.

Chapter II

CHRIST REVEALS THE NATURE OF GOD

Proofs of the Existence of God

The Bible nowhere attempts to prove the existence of God. Everywhere that fact is taken for granted, but from a time five hundred years before the birth of Christ the Greek philosophers had invented or discovered all the current proofs of theism (the doctrine of God's existence), except one (the ontological).

If these proofs are a part of the natural revelation of God, they certainly derive ultimately from Christ the revealer of God, and belong here. However, their value has been debated since the time of Immanuel Kant, the greatest modern metaphysician, who denied their validity. Kant was himself a believer in God, but he rejected the historic arguments for certain philosophical reasons.

My own opinion is that these proofs, or rather evidences, are true and hence valid for believers, but complete absence of the eyesight of faith would certainly make them less than demonstrative to unbelievers. Here we might re-echo the words of Jesus, "Blessed are the pure in heart for they shall see God." Viewing the subject from this standpoint we are doubtless justified theologically and even philosophically in saying that the only real and satisfactory proof of God is the inner experience of a pure heart. For the blind no demonstrative proof of the beauty of a painting exists.

Nevertheless, there are doubtless earnest students who have been caused by false arguments to doubt certain truths which are not doubtful and to deny spiritual facts which are un-

35

objectionable to men of the most brilliant genius. Doubtless any argument which clarifies such points is proper here.

The Ontological Proof

We take the only modern argument—and the most doubtful one—first. To state it properly would require too much space. Those who find it interesting should consult the authorities. In its simplest form it is the concept that the idea of the greatest, most perfect being must be true, as the idea of the most perfect being must include existence as one of its attributes. This idea has been developed by men like Descartes, Kant, and others. Following my thesis that all reason is one and its different products depend upon the nature of the data submitted either by the physical senses or by the spiritual senses, I will say that this ontological line of reasoning is essentially true, in spite of the logical defect that the insertion of an imaginary quality (like necessary existence) into an idea does not make that idea thereby factual. The evidence lies elsewhere.

Man has an intuition of a most perfect Being, at least of a Supreme Being. When he enshrines that idea even in such a theory as the ontological argument, he suffers frustration in its denial. It is obviously true, like the existence of the sky, though he cannot prove the sky to a blind man. Moreover this intuition of a Supreme Being creates a dilemma for all reasonable men: The Supreme Being exists for all normal human beings (at least, until they are blinded by sophistication). And He must be either of the highest moral character or the most evil moral character. It is impossible for a human being of average moral sensibilities to affirm the latter.

The Cosmological Argument

The argument from cause has always been one of the most highly esteemed arguments for the existence of God. The argument runs that every event must have a cause. This is an intuition of the human mind. It is impossible to conceive an eternal chain of causes and effects reaching back to infinity. If I cannot find in my house the source of the electric power causing my lights to burn, then I must trace that source back to the powerhouse. There must be a resting place for the mind in its search for causes. Throughout all time the most brilliant minds have rested in God as the First Cause. It would be futile to deny that skeptics have attacked this argument, much as a blind man, ignorant of art, might deny the beauty of Raphael's paintings. Space forbids a discussion here.

The Teleological Argument

The argument from design is another of the famous historical arguments which is also foolish to the spiritually blind, but which has approved itself to many of the greatest intellects of the race. It is worthy of elaborate treatment, as it gains in force by the vast mass of scientific facts which it can command. Recently I saw in a popular magazine a drawing showing how a certain flower was shaped ingeniously to pick up the pollen from the body of a bee which came only to gather the nectar of the flower. Such marvelous ingenuity of design is woven through the very web and woof of nature as to compel the assent of the mind to the proposition that one creative mind organized the entire fabric of the natural world, for it all fits together in a pattern so intricate and complex as to be convincing.

It would be naive to deny that skeptics have fought this argument with a thousand sophistries. They say this apparent interlocking is the end result of accidental contacts over millions of years; and they point out the apparent lack of such beneficent arrangements in certain unpleasant aspects of nature. We say in reply that if an explorer, traversing a new-found island in the firm belief that he is the first discoverer of the place, should suddenly find a watch, he would be forced to believe that some human being had been there before him. Even if all other evidence were lacking, he could not believe that natural forces alone could have produced such an ingenious contrivance as a watch. Neither can a normal man believe that this world with its rich provision for all man's need came by accident or by a "fortuitous combination of atoms," any more than he can believe that monkeys, playing with tons of type through ages of time, could accidentally cast them into the forms of Shakespeare's poems.

The Anthropological Argument

Sometimes called the moral argument or the argument from the nature of man, this reasoning goes that no fountain can rise higher than its source. Man exhibits qualities far superior to anything seen in nature aside from himself. Physically he is an animal. But even in his body he possesses "plus" qualities which justify his denying complete identity with the animals. Man's conscience justifies him in killing any animal for due cause, but he cannot kill a man, except under the most rigid of rationalistic arguments in justification of his act. The hand of man is fit for an artist or mechanic. His body is adapted to construct and inhabit vast sanitary communities. His mind is capable of creating science and civil law. And he has at once capacity for community living and ability to exist as a creative individual while yet loyal to his human community.

Above all he has conscience, a capacity which makes him aware of the majestic demands of moral law. This is right, and that is wrong; and he can do the wrong for a lifetime without ceasing to feel that the opposite course is right. There is a consciousness (conscience) within him which is also outside him and above him. This conscience is commanding. It cannot compel obedience, but it ceases not to inflict punishment for disobedience upon all but the most besotted and depraved of men. Even in them it sometimes awakens with a power which revolutionizes their lives. In all men from time to time it awakens yearnings for the good—the age-old hunger for God.

This superior constitution is evidence in itself of intelligence and moral character in the universe. We know these qualities are in the universe, for they are in us, and we are a part of the universe, and yet as we know these qualities in ourselves, we sense them as belonging primarily to another, higher than we.

To this argument belongs the fact of man's fear of death. It is possible to say that no animal has the fear of death as man has it. The animals fear danger and pain, but they do not know death, as man does. This fear of death is a telegraphic message to man out of eternity, apprising him of a reality beyond time. The yearnings of man's heart for God are also a kind of promise that help can be found.

Let no student think that these arguments are valueless because they require a special spiritual equipment to grasp them. Special equipment is necessary to appraise values in many fields, such as art, for example; or to understand questions in mathematics or the physical sciences, such as biochemistry or radiology. The arguments for the existence of God are not futile metaphysical speculations. On the contrary they amount to a demonstration when seen with the eyes of the heart, which Paul called "the eyes of your understanding" (Eph. 1:18).

In other words the affirmative judgments of spiritually qualified men are not purely subjective, but have the same objective rational validity as the findings of qualified thinkers in other areas—especially in the points wherein the spiritual thinkers agree, as in the unanimous belief in the existence of God.

It is no more unreasonable to require spiritual eyesight in those who would see God than it is to require trained eyesight in critics of painting.

THE NATURE OF GOD

Almost all the attributes of God treated in traditional theology were known and discussed by the Greek philosophers of the fifth century B.C. For this reason some modern biblical theologians prefer to ignore them altogether. It is our view that this is a technical treatise on theology, and therefore ought to include such topics.

In traditional theology the discussion of the attributes of

God is founded upon a metaphysical conception of God of incredible intricacy and complexity, and almost every famous theologian compiles his own catalogue, often ridiculing the other lists. Often the question is argued as to what is an attribute, and what not and why. We regard all this as outside the scope of true scriptural doctrine; hence we have simply given a list of qualities commonly attributed to God in the Bible itself. These only we regard as of the substance of scriptural doctrine.

The Unity of God

That God is one and not many is no matter of controversy in our modern Christianity. However, the importance of the unity of the Godhead for Christian theology demands the citation of some of the biblical evidence in its behalf: "We know that an idol is nothing in the world, and there is none other God but one" (I Cor. 8:4). "The Lord our God is one Lord" (Deut. 6:4). "The Lord he is God; there is none else beside him" (4:35). "Thou art God alone" (Ps. 86:10). "Thus saith the Lord, the King of Israel, and his redeemer the Lord of hosts; I am the first, and I am the last; and beside me there is no God" (Isa. 44:6).

This great truth is important to remember when we come to study about the existence of demons and the devil and Satan. There is no more room for a devil who is eternal than for any of the gods of heathenism. Here it is also important to remember that whatever a man exalts to supreme value in his life must become the god of his heart even if, theoretically he does acknowledge the Christian God as supreme. Such a person becomes an idolator. Paul said that covetousness is idolatry (Col. 3:5).

The Spirituality of God

It affords us a glimpse into the deep mystery of the universe that no man can properly tell what spirit is except by using figurative—that is metaphorical—language, for no man has

ever seen a spirit, just as no man has ever seen a thought. Yet
every man—and no animal—knows intuitively what a thought
is. Perhaps the easiest way to form a satisfactory concept of a
thought in everyday language is to think of the content of the
mind of man as existing on two lines which cross each other.
On the horizontal line we place matter and all physical phenomena, that is, the objects of taste, smell, touch, hearing, and
sight. Here, too, stand space, time, and number. On a line
which cuts this perpendicularly stand emotion: sadness, joy,
fear, grief, anxiety; the capacity to choose and will; the mental
and moral tastes, likes and dislikes, conscience, thought, spirit,
eternity, and God.

It should not be confusing that animals are given a low order
of consciousness both in this picture and in the real world.
John Wesley believed that the animals would be in heaven;
and there is nothing repulsive about the idea to us. Nevertheless, they do not share enough of the privileges of the eternal
sphere to bring them into the picture with man. These two
lines of matter and time and of thought and eternity exist in
man. God, however, exists on the plane of thought and of
eternity, in the realm of spirit. Spirit is the sole origin of
thought.

It is the testimony of Jesus Christ that "God is a Spirit"
(John 4:24). "A spirit hath not flesh and bones, as ye see me
have" (Luke 24:39). Therefore he is "the invisible God" (Col.
1:15). He is "the God of the spirits of all flesh" (Num. 16:22).
"Who only hath immortality; . . . whom no man hath seen, nor
can see" (I Tim. 6:16) does not mean that God cannot create
man as an immortal creature, for that he does. But God is the
supreme Spirit who has immortality as his nature and not as a
gift. The fact that God is spirit is the basis for two other statements concerning him: God is life, and God is personality.

God is life. He alone is the source of our physical, as of our
immortal life.

God is personality. Personality involves the possession of
intellect, He is "the only wise God" (Tim. 1:17); and emotion,

"God is love" (I John 4:8); and will, "This is the will of God" (I Thess. 4:3). The notion that personality degrades the nature of God is derived from the ancient Greek philosophy which denied love to the nature of God. There is no space to combat this pagan folly here; enough to say it contradicts the words of Jesus Christ that "God so loved the world." Human personality has the three aspects of intellect, emotion, and will. God's personality might have more aspects of which we cannot even dream. His must be above man's personality, as the stars are above the earth. But it cannot be less than the personality of man. To say so is to dishonor God and to degrade him beneath man. The personality of God has self-direction—the realm of freedom in which miracles are possible—and self-consciousness—the realm of transcendence in which all miracles must occur.

The Eternity of God

The Bible reveals to us the God "which is, and which was, and which is to come, the Almighty" (Rev. 1:8). He is "the King eternal" (I Tim. 1:17). God overrides time just as he stands above the world of matter. According to one definition, time is the measure of motion in matter. Before the creation of matter, therefore, there was no time; and time shall cease to be when matter ceases to exist. But the life of God arches from the eternity before creation to the eternity beyond creation: "From everlasting to everlasting, thou art God" (Ps. 90:2). Here the Hebrew word for "everlasting" is *olam,* which may without violence be translated "eternity."

However, all this does not mean that the eternal life which God lives and which his children share with him is without event. The Book of Revelation portrays (figuratively, of course, but necessarily truthfully) life as proceeding along a course of ecstatic and glorious enjoyment. Time shall cease when matter ceases; but what about the eternal motion of the divine will and energy sustaining and guiding his people in eternity? Will not that involve a spiritual analogue of material motion and its shadow, time? Some theologians say, Yes. We shall wait and see.

The eternal life in which God lives, transcending earthly time, does not cut God off from the time order of the world and limit him to existence in an eternal now, where the past, present, and future are indistinguishable. If God is perfect in wisdom, as we must believe, then he knows fully the meaning of time to us. He understands our past, present, and future as well as we do and infinitely better.

The Self-Sufficiency of God

God says of himself: "I am the first, and I am the last, and beside me there is no God" (Isa. 44:6). "Before me there was no God formed" (43:10). These texts set forth the character of the Christian God whom metaphysics attempts to designate by such terms as the Absolute and the Unconditioned. These are not scriptural terms, for at the very instant when God determined to create creatures with the power of choice such as men are, at that moment he chose to put a certain limitation on himself. Hence in Scripture, God is never the Unconditioned. At the same time we would reject the modern theory of a finite God. He is the loving Father.

The Immutability of God

"I am the Lord, I change not" (Mal. 3:6). "Jesus Christ the same yesterday, today, and forever" (Heb. 13:8). "Thou, Lord, in the beginning hast laid the foundation of the earth; and the heavens are the work of thine hands: they shall perish; but thou remainest; . . . thou art the same, and thy years shall not fail" (1:10-12).

This immutability of God simply means that the divine nature does not grow or change. It neither declines nor progresses. But this does not mean that God does not change what we might call the tactics of his battle against Satan. In reality the God of eternal wisdom does not stand like a stone in the ebb and tide of human history, but in infinite wisdom he reacts instantaneously in approval or disapproval of every act of every tiny atom in the vast sea of human life. The immutability of God means that he always reacts in the same way to the same acts or circumstances throughout all the centuries of time.

The Perfection of God

"Be ye therefore perfect, even as your father in heaven is perfect" (Matt. 5:48). The context indicates that the perfection in God here indicated is the perfection in love which the eternal Father is most anxious to impart to his children. Otherwise God is so complete, so exalted, and so perfect that we may not even compare with him those excellencies by which we measure perfection.

The Freedom of God

One of the sharpest differences between speculative theology and biblical theology is that the former thinks of God as the Absolute, so bound by his perfections that he has no choices left in dealing with the contingencies which arise from the actions of his free creatures. Over against all this supposed bondage of the behavior of Infinity, the Bible sets the God and Father of our Lord Jesus Christ, "who worketh all things after the counsel of his own will" (Eph. 1:11). God was under no compulsion to create the world, and he is under no necessity to sustain it. Its order and seeming uniformity is only the result of the exercise of his own free will.

The Omnipotence of God

Fifty-three times in the King James Version of the Bible God is called "the Almighty." "With God all things are possible" (Mark 10:27). "There is nothing too hard for thee" (Jer. 32:17).

Many foolish questions have been raised concerning this subject: Can God cause a thing to be and not to be at the same time? and so on. To all these the answer is that God can do whatever he wills to do, but it is "impossible for God to lie" (Heb. 6:18); for "God . . . cannot lie" (Titus 1:2). God cannot do anything contrary to his character, and he is strong enough never to be under compulsion to do anything contrary to his will. "And this is the confidence that we have in him, that, if we ask anything according to his will, he heareth us" (I John 5:14). God will never do anything foolish, ridiculous, or unreasonable.

The Omnipresence of God

"Whither shall I go from thy spirit? or whither shall I flee from thy presence? If I ascend up into heaven, thou art there: if I make my bed in hell, behold, thou art there. If I take the wings of the morning, and dwell in the uttermost parts of the sea; even there shall thy hand lead me, and thy right hand shall hold me" (Ps. 139:7-10).

It is important to distinguish this doctrine from pantheism. In pantheism, God is present everywhere as a constituent part of the nature of the world. In Christianity God is not part of the world. He stands over against the universe as something other than it. Moreover, God is Spirit. He is not extended in space any more than a thought may be extended in space. God is everywhere in the created universe by reason of his perfect knowledge and his perfect power. But he specially manifests his presence in heaven. "It is God's throne" (Matt. 5:34). He likewise specially manifests his presence in the hearts of his people. "I dwell in the high and holy place, with him also that is of a contrite and humble spirit" (Isa. 57:15). "Where two or three are gathered together in my name, there am I in the midst of them" (Matt. 18:20).

The Omniscience of God

"O the depth of the riches both of the wisdom and knowledge of God! how unsearchable are his judgments, and his ways past finding out! For who hath known the mind of the Lord? or who hath been his counselor?" (Rom. 11:33-34). "Great is our Lord, and of great power: his understanding is infinite" (Ps. 147:5). "The eyes of the Lord are in every place, beholding the evil and the good" (Prov. 15:3). "Known unto God are all his works from the beginning of the world" (Acts 15:18). This includes foreknowledge of all things. "Behold, the former things are come to pass, and new things do I declare; before they spring forth, I tell you of them" (Isa. 42:9).

God's foreknowledge is the basis for predictive prophecy. That concept is certainly true, but how is it to be understood? The famous passage usually supposed to nail down predestination immovably certainly admits of a conditional predestination: "Whom he did foreknow, he also did predestinate to be conformed to the image of his Son" (Rom. 8:29). Undoubtedly the meaning of this text is that we have not come uninvited and uncared for, like homeless strangers, into this world. God thought on us with love and predestinated every human being to a place in his favor, before any of us were born into this world. Some have rejected this predestined favor and love. In other words, modern scholarship has shown that "to know" a person in biblical language often indicates more than simply intellectual apprehension. Sometimes it denotes love: "The Lord knoweth the way of the righteous" (Ps. 1:6). Christ says of his sheep: "I know them, and they follow me" (John 10:27).

But if God knows all things, does he know the name and person of every human being who will be damned, likewise the exact time and means of their damnation? Most Christian theologians say, Yes. But they teach that this foreknowledge of God has no compulsive effect upon the event itself, any more than my past knowledge of the treason of Benedict Arnold involves me in that act of treason. Possibly so.

However, some of the most brilliant minds of the church have reasoned as follows: God knows all knowledge, but the contingent act of an utterly free human will which is to function on July 1, 2089, is not a factor of any kind of knowledge. It does not exist at all. It is not merely the human unknown, but the absolutely nonexistent. As such it is not a subject of knowledge, and lack of knowledge of it is by no means ignorance. We leave this question open, inclining to the view that, undoubtedly man's will is free, but no human teacher is under obligation to dispel all mystery concerning it.

The Wisdom of God

"O Lord, how manifold are thy works! in wisdom hast thou made them all: the earth is full of thy riches" (Ps. 104:24). "With him is wisdom and strength, he hath counsel and understanding" (Job 12:13). Wisdom is the ability to utilize knowledge skillfully, to act intelligently, to apply reason to the utmost; but always with overtones of moral value and intent.

God's wisdom is revealed in the plan of salvation: "Wherein he hath abounded toward us in all wisdom and prudence" (Eph. 1:8), and wherein is revealed "Christ the power of God, and the wisdom of God" (I Cor. 1:24).

The Goodness and Holiness of God

"The Lord is good to all: and his tender mercies are over all his works" (Ps. 145:9). "The goodness of God leadeth thee to repentance" (Rom. 2:4). In God's goodness are based his benevolence, mercy, and grace.

In heaven the hosts around the throne cry: "Holy, holy, holy, Lord God Almighty, which was, and is, and is to come" (Rev. 4:8). To understand the holiness of God, we must remember that originally the term "holy" meant "that which belongs to God." It was a long growth of religious insight which led to the conviction that the man who belongs to God must possess a moral excellence like that of God himself. However, we do not understand the primary meaning of the holiness of God to be moral excellence regarded only as a static quality; rather the holiness of God is a divine possessiveness which follows man through all the highways of history and up past the tragedy of the cross in order to possess man completely and in reality. This is by no means a denial of the moral excellence of God but a further affirmation of the manner in which that moral excellency shows itself dynamic.

Throughout all the Christian dispensation God is demanding: "Be ye holy; for I am holy" (I Pet. 1:16).

The Justice of God

The justice of God is a theme of vast extent. "Great and marvelous are thy works, Lord God Almighty; just and true are thy ways, thou King of saints" (Rev. 15:3). "Justice and judgment are the habitation of thy throne: mercy and truth shall go before thy face" (Ps. 89:14). He is the one "Who without respect of persons judgeth according to every man's work" (I Pet. 1:17). This monolithic rock of the justice of God stands like a Gibraltar above all the stormy seas of history. The man who regards it from the side of disobedience cannot avoid the conviction that for him the justice of God is indeed the wrath of God.

The Love of God

"God is love" (I John 4:8). That love is the basis of our redemption: "God so loved the world that he gave his only begotten Son" (John 3:16). "Herein is love, not that we loved God, but that he loved us, and sent his Son to be the propitiation for our sins" (I John 4:10).

The principal New Testament word for love in the Greek is *agape*. God is *agape*. Human love often regards its object as that which can bring benefit to the lover. But the divine *agape* pursues the beloved in order to confer a benefit. The holiness of God pursues us because he would regain what is originally his own. The love of God follows us in order that that which God's holiness has reclaimed for itself may be "filled with all the fullness of God" (Eph. 3:19).

CHRIST REVEALS A TRIUNE GOD

The first preaching of the gospel was free from all philosophical definitions, but when the church met with Greek philosophy, there arose and continued for centuries a perfect agony in the mind of Christian teachers to interpret the facts of the Christian message so as to make them agreeable to reason. Thus many seemingly contradictory statements were made about Christ. He was man, born of a woman, and yet the apostolic preaching set him forth as possessed of the attributes of God. The long mental ferment finally produced, after many efforts, the Niceno-Constantinopolitan Creed in 381, stating the doctrine of the Trinity (including the deity of Christ) in the form which has prevailed in all branches of the Christian church—Eastern Orthodox, Roman, and Protestant.

The Protestant statement of that faith is well and authoritatively declared in the Westminster Confession of 1647: "In the unity of the God-head there be three persons, of one substance, power, and eternity: God the Father, God the Son, and God the Holy Ghost" (Chap. II: Sec. III).

This remarkable doctrine is famous, not only for its incomprehensible mystery, but even more for the fact that despite its difficulty and its capacity to stimulate debate, it is perhaps the most unanimously accepted creed of universal historic Christianity. Literally tens of thousands of the most brilliant men of genius of all ages and of all races have joined in hailing this creed as the fundamental truth of Christianity. We state this historic fact, not to compel assent to authority, but to apprise students of the responsibility a rebel must take if he attempts to destroy this foundation stone of the Christian faith. It is not too much to say that, true or false, this doctrine is by every test nothing more nor less than historic Christianity itself.

Christ, of course, is the key to the doctrine of the Trinity. Most standard works on theology contain long and labored arguments to prove the deity of each of the Persons in the divine Trinity, but we can save ourselves much labor by remembering that not only historically but logically Christ is the key to the whole discussion. Historically, it was the gigantic battle over the place of Christ in Christian theology which, so to speak, forced the way to a seat on the throne of God for the

Galilean Carpenter; only then was it found impossible to deny a like honor to the Holy Spirit.

Even the Old Testament hints of the Trinity. The first word for God in the Old Testament is the Hebrew word for God, *Elohim,* which is plural. Liberals regard this as a relic of polytheism in the Old Testament. Orthodox Jews see in its plural form a reflection of the kingly majesty of God, after the pattern of the Semitic languages but conservative Christians see here also a hint of the divine Trinity which is basic to the nature of God. The same reflections apply to the verse, "Let us make man in our image" (Gen. 1:26). The three who here conferred were God the Father who says: "I have made the earth, and created man upon it" (Isa. 45:12); God the Son of whom John says: "All things were made by him" (1:3); and the "Spirit of God" who "moved" over the ancient chaos of unfinished creation (Gen. 1:2). Three men stood by Abraham, when "the Lord appeared unto him" (Gen. 18:1-2). The priestly blessing in Numbers 6:24-26 is triune in form. "And in heaven the angels greet the throne with three ascriptions of holiness" (Isa. 6:3). "And now the Lord God, and his Spirit hath sent me" (Isa. 48:16).

There is evidence that the angel of God in the Old Testament was a manifestation of God. When Jacob wrestled with the angel, he afterwards said that he had seen God face to face (Gen. 32:30). Isaiah saw the Lord upon a throne, and immediately prophesied (6:1-12). John quotes Isaiah's prophecy and adds: "These things said Esaias, when he saw his [Christ's] glory and spake of him" (12:41). This passage warrants us in finding the pre-existent Christ in most of the appearances of the angel of God, and even of Jehovah, in the Old Testament. Thus God said: "Behold I send an Angel before thee, to keep thee in the way, and to bring thee into the place which I have prepared. Beware of him, and obey his voice, provoke him not; . . . for my name is in him" (Exod. 23:20-21).

"The Lord hath said unto me, Thou art my Son; this day

have I begotten thee" (Ps. 2:7). This line of evidence used to be popular in ancient Christianity (and in the New Testament, too), but liberal scholars have taken guidance from non-Christian interpreters to obviate much of this interpretation. Personally, I think it is valid.

THE DEITY OF CHRIST

The deity of Christ is proved by his pre-existence. John the Baptist said: "He that cometh after me is preferred before me: for he was before me" (John 1:15). "What and if ye shall see the Son of man ascend up where he was before?" (6:62). "Before Abraham was, I am" (8:58). "The glory which I had with thee before the world was. . . . Thou lovedst me before the foundation of the world" (17:5, 24). Here we find Christ mentioned as existing not only before his birth but before the creation of the world.

New Testament Messianic Prophecies

In the following texts we are not concerned with what liberal scholars think of the Old Testament texts cited. Rather our argument rests entirely on the view of these texts taken by the New Testament writers, which view we must regard as authoritative in this connection. Please read the entire selection indicated in each case. We give only the clue words, for brevity. "I said, O my God, take me not away in the midst of my days . . ." (Ps. 102:24-27). The author of Hebrews applies this passage with Psalm 45:6-7 to Christ. "But unto the Son, he saith, Thy throne, O God, is forever" (Heb. 1:8-12). "His name shall be called . . . the mighty God" (Isa. 9:1-7). Part of this great messianic passage is cited by Matthew and applied to Christ (4:12-16). Isaiah wrote: "Of the increase of his government . . . there shall be no end . . . upon the throne of David (9:7). Also, "Make straight in the desert a highway for our God." (40:3). Matthew (3:1-3) applies this to the ministry of John the Baptist preparing the way for Christ, who therefore must be God. "Look unto me, and be ye saved, all the ends of the earth; for I am God. . . . Unto me every knee shall bow" (Isa. 45:22-23). Paul applies this passage to Christ: "We shall all stand before the judgment seat of Christ. For it is written, . . . Every knee shall bow to me, and every tongue shall confess to God." Read Romans 14:10-12. Here Paul identified Christ with God.

"The Lord said unto my Lord, Sit thou at my right hand" (Ps. 110:1). Christ applied this verse to himself. When the Jews replied to his question, "Whose son is the Christ?" with the statement that Christ was the Son of David, he quoted Psalm 110:1 and asked, "If David then call him Lord, how is he his Son?" (Matt. 22:41-45). The Jews refused to pronounce the sacred name of God, Jehovah, or Yahweh, pronouncing it *Adonai,* or Lord, instead. For them, Lord and God were equal. "Sanctify the Lord of Hosts . . . and he shall be . . . for a stone of stumbling and a rock of offense" (Isa. 8:13-15). This is applied to Christ in I Peter 2:7-8. Joel's words, "And it shall come to pass, that whosoever shall call on the name of the Lord shall be delivered" (2:32), are applied to Christ in Acts 2:21 and in First Corinthians: "With all that in every place call upon the name of Jesus Christ our Lord" (1:2). "Behold, I will send my messenger . . . and the Lord, whom ye seek, shall suddenly come to his temple" (Mal. 3:1). This is applied to Christ in Matthew 11:10; Mark 1:2-3; Luke 7:26-27. Christ is the Lord here.

Christ Is Called God

"In the beginning was the Word, and the Word was with God, and the Word was God" (John 1:1). "Of whom as concerning the flesh Christ came who is over all God blessed forever amen" (Rom. 9:5). Here I have omitted the punctuation, as there is no punctuation in the Greek text. "We are in him that is true, even in his Son Jesus Christ. This is the true God, and eternal life" (I John 5:20). "And he that sat upon the throne, said, . . . I am Alpha and Omega. . . . I will be his God" (Rev. 21:5-8). But Christ is the Alpha and Omega.

"Behold, I come quickly. . . . I am Alpha and Omega" (22:12-13). "And Thomas answered and said unto him: My Lord and my God" (John 20:28). Here an apostle calls Christ, God. Paul says: "Looking for that blessed hope, and the glorious appearing of the great God and our Savior Jesus Christ" (Titus 2:13). Anyone familiar with the Hebrew idiom of repetition would think at once that this is an example of such repetition. The great God is our Savior, Jesus Christ.

Elsewhere in the New Testament the epiphania [manifestations of God] are never used of the Father, but only of Christ. "But unto the Son he saith, Thy throne, O God is forever and ever" (Heb. 1:8). Here Christ is called God. Christ is "the King of Israel" (John 1:49), "the Lord of glory" (I Cor. 2:8). Christ is repeatedly called the Son of God in the Scripture, and Jesus blessed Peter for having received that revelation (Matt. 16:18).

Christ Possesses the Attributes of God

Christ has every attribute of God (John 16:15; Col. 2:9). He has eternal existence and is omnipotent (Isa. 9:6; Phil. 3:21). He is immutable (Heb. 1:10-12). He is omniscient (John 2:24-25; 21:17; Col. 2:3; Rev. 2:23). He is omnipresent (Matt. 18:20; 28:20; John 3:13). He performs the works of God. He is Creator: "All things were made by him; and without him was not anything made that was made" (John 1:3). "For by him were all things created, that are in heaven, and that are in earth, visible and invisible, whether they be thrones, or dominions, or principalities, or powers: all things were created by him, and for him: and he is before all things, and by him all things consist" (Col. 1:16-17). "And in him all things hold together" (RSV).

Christ controls the providential government of the world (Matt. 28:18; Luke 10:22; John 3:35; 17:2; Acts 10:36; Rom. 14:9; Eph. 1:22; Col. 1:17; Heb. 1:3; Rev. 17:14). He forgives sins (Matt. 9:2-7; Mark 2:7-10; Col. 3:13). He will raise the dead and judge all men (John 5:22, 25-30; Phil. 3:20-21; Matt.

25:31-32; Acts 10:42; 17:31; Rom. 14:10; II Tim. 4:1). Divine worship was paid to Christ by the New Testament saints and apostles (Luke 24:51-52; Acts 1:24; 2:21; 7:59-60; Rom. 10: 12-13; I Cor. 1:2; II Cor. 12:8-9; I Thess. 3:11-13; II Thess. 2:16-17). He is worshiped by angels (Heb. 1:6). He is worshiped by every creature in the universe (Rom. 14:11; Phil. 2:9-11; Rev. 5:13-14).

THE COMPLETE HUMANITY OF CHRIST

It is fundamental to the doctrine of Christ to bear in mind constantly his complete and perfect humanity. "Let this mind be in you, which was also in Christ Jesus: who, being in the form of God, thought it not robbery to be equal with God: but made himself of no reputation, and took upon him the form of a servant, and was made in the likeness of men: and being found in fashion as a man, he humbled himself, and became obedient unto death, even the death of the cross" (Phil. 2:5-9).

The historic Christian doctrine is that in Christ there is one person; in the unity of his person, two natures—the divine and the human; and that there is no change or mixture or confusion of these two natures, but that each retains its own distinguishing properties. "The Word was made flesh." "The church of God . . . purchased by his own blood." "He bore our sins in his own body on the tree." "A spirit hath not flesh and bones as ye see me have."

It was inevitable that heresies concerning the person of Christ should arise. Sabellius was an African presbyter who lived about the middle of the third century. He maintained that the appellations, Father, Son, and Holy Spirit, were only so many different manifestations and names of one and the same divine Being, who was Father in the Old Testament, Son in the New Testament, and Holy Spirit in the present age. This heresy has been revived as the "Jesus only" doctrine of our own time. Arius (280-336), a presbyter of Alexandria, Egypt, taught that Christ was the first of all created beings, but yet a creature, and not God. His doctrine was revived by Socinus in the sixteenth century.

THE DEITY OF THE HOLY SPIRIT

Since everywhere and in all time whosoever has admitted the deity of Christ has also accepted the deity of the Holy Spirit, not so much space is required for that subject. Nevertheless, the work of the Spirit is so essential in the matter of our salvation that all Christians should feel a deep concern to learn all that it is possible to know about him. Although the Greek word for spirit is in the neuter gender in the New Testament, nevertheless personal pronouns are often applied to the Holy Ghost, as in John 14:16-17, 26; 16:7, 14-15. He is spoken of as Comforter, Instructor, Patron, Guide, Advocate. He has personal qualities: intelligence and will. He may be resisted, grieved, blasphemed, lied to, and tempted. He performs personal acts. He strives, speaks, guides, intercedes, works miracles; he sanctifies, sends forth messengers, distributes gifts, seals. Divine names are given him as in Acts 5:3-4. He is credited with divine attributes: omnipresence, omnipotence, eternity. He is credited with doing the works of God: creation (Gen. 1:2), regeneration (John 3:5-6), the resurrection of the dead (I Pet. 3:18; Rom. 8:11). He is worshiped (Rom. 9:1; II Cor. 13:14; Matt. 28:19).

THE WORKS OF GOD

God Created the World

"Through faith we understand that the worlds were framed by the word of God" (Heb. 11:3). "In the beginning God created the heaven and the earth" (Gen. 1:1). "Thou, even thou, art Lord alone; thou hast made heaven, the heaven of heavens, with all their host, the earth and all things that are therein, the seas, and all that is therein, and thou preservest them all" (Neh. 9:6).

For every thoughtful person, every statement of fact is a brier patch of questions, and the biblical account of creation is no less.

Creation is the free act of the Omnipotent calling into existence all the creatures both physical and spiritual of the entire universe, without the use of pre-existent matter or spirit outside himself—the bringing into being of all that is not God.

God says: "Bring my sons from far, and my daughters from the ends of the earth; even every one that is called by my name: for I have created him for my glory" (Isa. 43:6-7).

Here it is expressly stated that the human race was created that God might delight in "bringing many sons unto glory" (Heb. 2:10). Christ's great prayer for his church implored, "I will that they also, whom thou hast given me, be with me where I am; that they may behold my glory" (John 17:24).

There is an ancient theory that matter has coexisted alongside of God from all eternity and that the act of creation was simply the work of fashioning this matter into definite form. This the Christian doctrine denies: "Things which are seen were not made of things which do appear" (Heb. 11:3). The Son of God is declared to be "before all things" (Col. 1:17).

We regard it as generally a mistake to try to support the Word of God by the evidences of science. Science changes so rapidly, and, moreover, it takes science so long to catch up with the Bible. At the moment of this writing, however, after ages of debate, a majority of the best scientists have agreed that the universe had a beginning in time. (Part of this conclusion rests upon the new science of radiology.)

God Preserves His Universe

One need not be an evolutionist to observe the continual changes in nature. These changes have given rise to the question of the basis for the continuance of the natural order. Some theologians profess belief in a continuous creation wherein God is eternally wrestling with chaotic matter and bringing it into form. This doctrine is too harmonious with idealism, or even with pantheism. Pantheism is the doctrine that the universe and God are identical. They are two aspects of one reality and stand to each other like right and left. This philosophy, I believe, is the greatest future foe of Christianity. Idealism is akin to pantheism. It teaches the nonreality of matter. Matter is a dream projected before our eyes by the power of God.

Another theory of the upholding of matter is that furnished by deism, which holds that God fitted the world with natural forces as a watchmaker does a watch—wound it up, and went off and left it. He is an absentee God. A better doctrine is that of the new Testament where we read of Christ as "upholding all things by the word of his power" (Heb. 1:3). Also Nehemiah 9:6, quoted above, assures us that God preserves all things. "Behold the fowls of the air: . . . your heavenly Father feedeth them. . . . Consider the lilies. . . . Wherefore, if God so clothe the grass of the field . . . (Matt. 6:26-30).

THE PROVIDENCE OF GOD

Closely akin to the subject of creation is the Christian doctrine of the providence of God. But before studying this subject it is necessary to consider two phases of the divine existence known as "immanence" and "transcendence." While these are philosophical terms, they describe so accurately scriptural aspects of the divine relation to the world, that we prefer to explain rather than ignore them.

The Divine Immanence

The divine immanence means the divine indwelling in nature. Paul certainly taught the divine immanence in his sermon on Mars' Hill: "For in him we live, and move, and have our being" (Acts 17:28). "Do not I fill heaven and earth? saith the Lord" (Jer. 23:24). In fact the doctrine of the divine immanence is indistinguishable from the doctrine of the divine omnipresence, and we believe its basis is the same; namely, God lives in the natural world by his omniscience and by his omnipotence. This distinction is necessary to save us from the identification of nature and God which is pantheism. His immanence is also the means by which God preserves all nature. This divine supervision of nature is in accordance with the order of nature revealed to Noah: "While the earth remaineth, seedtime and harvest, and cold and heat, and summer and winter, and day and night shall not cease" (Gen. 8:22). "He made a decree for the rain" (Job 28:26). While God is not subject to the finite relations of man, it will clarify our thought to compare the immanence of God with man's sympathetic nervous system which works automatically without conscious personal supervision and effort.

The Divine Transcendence

Likewise we liken the transcendence of God to man's self-consciousness—which instead of being bound by uniform natural law is constantly rising above physical necessity and acting in voluntary freedom at every step of the way. This freedom which man enjoys, we insist, cannot be denied to God because he has made laws for nature.

Within this realm of transcendence lies the supernatural, which is only another name for the divine transcendence, self-consciousness, and freedom. Here also is the realm of prayer and of miracle. In fact whatever takes place in this realm is miracle. We say this in opposition to the ancient theory that miracle must be something extraordinary whenever it occurs. We maintain that in the realm of the divine transcendence everything which happens is a miracle.

General and Special Providence

Many theologians place the divine preservation of the world under the category of general providence. This we cannot do, as we regard the divine preservation of nature as coming under the rule of the immanent God, while all providence is superintended by the miracle-working transcendent God. This definition removes the distinction between general and special providence. All providence is general and special at all times. It is general as extending to all men, and it is special as concerned with the most intimate details of man's existence. "The very hairs of your head are all numbered" (Matt. 10:30).

For the ungodly, this providential care is intended for their salvation. "The goodness of God leadeth thee to repentance" (Rom. 2:4). For the believer all the circumstances of life combine together for his eternal welfare: "We know that in everything God works for good with those who love him, who are called according to his purpose" (Rom. 8:28, RSV). Pages of texts teach this doctrine in both the Old and New Testaments. These texts were written to strengthen faith, but they will prove stumbling blocks if they are read as promises to exempt the saints from suffering rather than as assurances that they will be able to endure it.

God sees with equal ease both sides of the screen of eternity, and he has regard for our happiness "in the ages to come." Paul reckoned that "the sufferings of this present time are not worthy to be compared with the glory which shall be revealed in us" (Rom. 8:18). And unless we gain his spiritual viewpoint, we shall gain nothing but frustration from the multitude of assurances concerning the divine providence. In our moments of weakness the enemy can quote them with astounding power. Furthermore, it must be remembered that these promises may well be given to encourage us to lay hold on them in prayer. For although most Christians regard them as somewhat automatic—and such they indeed seem to be—nevertheless, there is reason to believe that much benefit could be derived from them by pleading them before God in the prayer of faith.

ANGELS

The Creation of Angels

At this point we must bring our minds up sharply with the radical assurance that all things in heaven and earth which are not God were brought into existence by the creative fiat that made the universe. "For by him were all things created, that are in heaven, and that are in earth, visible and invisible" (Col. 1:16). The angels differ from men in that they were each created individually. There are multitudes of them: "ten thousand times ten thousand, and thousands of thousands" (Rev. 5:11). They are not all equal. The thrones and dominions, principalities, and powers of Colossians 1:16 are believed by conservative theologians to belong to the angels. There are princes among them (Dan. 12:1). Yet they are not to be worshiped (Rev. 22:8-9). We read of holy angels, and since God could not create them evil we are compelled to believe they are all created holy.

The Fall of the Angels

In the early days of our work our ministers were diligent in combating premillennialism, especially as it developed at that time in Seventh Day Adventism. Among the features of this doctrine was the theory of a literal battle in the very heaven of the throne of God where the angels of God fought to expel foul demons from the throne room of God. In conducting this argument some of our older ministers were driven to the extreme of denying the fall of the angels. We regard this battle in heaven as entirely figurative. Nevertheless, the Scriptures plainly teach that some of the angels fell. Moreover the existence of demons and of Satan cannot otherwise be accounted for.

Undoubtedly the newly created angels were placed on probation, for some of them fell. For "God spared not the angels that sinned, but cast them down to hell, and delivered them into chains of darkness, to be reserved unto judgment. Undoubtedly these chains of darkness are not literal bonds which limit or confine their movements to hell. They are chains of guilt which, nevertheless, permit them to traverse the earth seeking whom they may devour (I Pet. 5:8). Again we read: "And the angels which kept not their first estate, but left their own habitation, he hath reserved in everlasting chains under darkness unto the judgment of the great day (Jude 6). Of this mighty host of angels who sinned, Satan was the prince or leader, and doubtless there are hundreds of such demonic leaders of the evil powers of darkness. Like wicked men they lost their privilege through transgression, while their associates who were true to God, passed the test of probation and were promoted to be holy angels in heaven.

PART TWO

THE WORK OF CHRIST AS PRIEST

Chapter III

MAN'S NEED OF CHRIST, THE SAVIOR

"For such an high priest became us, who is holy, harmless, undefiled, separate from sinners, and made higher than the heavens" (Heb. 7:26).

"Thou shalt call his name Jesus [Joshua] for he shall save his people from their sins" (Matt. 1:21).

THEORIES OF THE NATURE OF SIN

Popular Ideas About Sin

A belief in two eternal forces of good and evil prevailed in ancient Persia where Zoroaster represented Ormuzd as the good god and Ahriman as the bad god and author of all evil. These gods are naturally in eternal conflict. Many variations of this theory have arisen.

Some believe that sin is due to human limitations and involvement in sinful society. This theory is that any creature less than infinite must of necessity fall short of the perfection required by the infinite God. This theory is widely held by Christians who teach that no one can live above sin.

The theory that sin is due to life in the body of human flesh has many forms, but it most certainly comes down to us from the ancient Greek philosophy which taught that the soul is a pure, bright-shining thing which is always contaminated by association with the earthly body, whereas Scripture teaches that the contamination of the body comes from the soul. "For out of the heart proceed evil thoughts, murders: . . . these are the things which defile a man" (Matt. 15:19-20). The Apostle Paul commonly uses the term "flesh," not to indicate that the human flesh is the source of sin, but as a technical name for the sinful nature of mankind.

Sin is the abuse of freedom. It is impossible to believe that sin is a necessity of man's being or a necessary step in his progress to higher realms of perfection. Sin arises out of a wrong choice which man is allowed to make because he is free.

A Dogmatic Definition of Sin

The Westminster Shorter Catechism (1647) defines sin thus: "Sin is any want of conformity unto, or transgression of, the law of God" (Ques. 14).

It is easy to see that this Calvinistic creed makes it impossible for any, however saintly, to live free from sin, for how could any person be wise enough to know that he was not in anything falling short of the ideal law of God in the smallest iota of one of its statutes? Therefore, Wesleyans have amended this definition as follows: "Sin is any rebellious want of conformity unto, or willful transgression of, the known law of God." No earnest Christian is wise enough to fulfill the first version, and no sincere Christian dare live below the second version, of this definition.

Before his vision of the sheet let down at Joppa, Peter was violating the first version of this definition of sin, for he was guilty of a lack of conformity to the law of God by failing to preach to the Gentiles. How many Christians have been guilty of a lack of conformity to the law of God through the practice of unconscious race prejudice?

New Testament Concept of Sin

The Greek New Testament uses several terms for sin. *Hamartia* is the most common, occurring no less than 158 times. Literally it means to miss the mark. *Adikia,* occurring 66 times, means injustice or unrighteousness. *Paraptoma,* a falling away, or a misstep, appears 23 times. *Anomia*, disobedience to the divine law, or antilaw, occurs 23 times; *asebeia*, ungodliness or irreverence, 17 times; *parabasis*, a false step, transgression, 12 times. These are the principal terms used in the Greek Testament to describe sin. These terms all indicate some kind of maladjustment, a deviation from a goal, a failure to reach one's objective. Others are *epithumea*, lust or concupiscense; *echthiaeistheon*, enmity against God; *ta heauton zetein*, seeking one's own; and *poneria*, evil.

The Bible teaching is in the thought forms of the ancient East—personal. The Oriental, and especially the tribesman, is, of course, bound by the immemorial customs of his race, but above all rules and statutes, he stands in the immediate personal relation of loyalty to his lord, be he chief or king. He may not know, or even be able to read, the statutes. Likely as not there are no written statutes. But he knows what kind of man his chief wishes him to be. However, this personal loyalty is not found merely in uncivilized states of culture. It is the fundamental basis of God's law to men.

When Jesus was demanded to cite the greatest commandment, he quoted a passage which melted all statutes into a principle of love for God: "Thou shalt love the Lord thy God with all thy heart . . . and thy neighbor as thyself" (Mark 12:30-31). According to this, the law of God is not a set of ten thousand statutes, three fourths of which a man may not know or understand. The law of God is to live in love. Therefore, sin is the act which evinces lack of love for God or for man. Also sin is the condition of living outside that love. The Apostle John summed it up by saying: "Sin is the transgression of the law." In the Greek it reads "Sin is *anomia*" (lawlessness, or antilaw). This is a fair description of that which might be either an act or a state.

Sin is both an act and a state. We are all familiar with the acts of sin which draw down both the wrath of the civil law and of God. But we are not always fully aware of the state of sin out of which the acts of sin grow. It is the duty of the civil law to count all men innocent until proved guilty. But common sense teaches us that there is a life of lawlessness which constantly generates evil deeds.

THE NATURE OF MAN

The races of man are one. God "hath made of one blood all nations of men" (Acts 17:26). "By one man sin entered into the world" (Rom. 5:12). Man is body and spirit: "And they stoned Stephen, calling upon God, and saying, Lord Jesus, receive my spirit." God "breathed the breath of life into his nostrils, and he became a living soul" (Gen. 2:27). In the New Testament, spirit is the higher part of human consciousness, and soul, psyche, is the lower range of consciousness. In other words, there is one spirit in man, and the lower range of that spirit, concerned with the functioning of the animal life, is the soul—if we make any distinction.

Whence came man's spirit? There are three theories as to how a man receives his soul: (1) Creationism. Each soul is created afresh with the generation of every individual. (2) Pre-existence. Every soul of humanity was alive and pre-existent in eternity before birth. (3) Traducianism. Each soul of man comes into existence upon the generation of every new individual and is an inheritance from its ancestors, the same as his body. This is the doctrine we hold.

Man Was Created Holy

"Lo, this only have I found, that God hath made man upright; but they have sought out many inventions" (Eccles. 7:29). Man's life was derived from God, hence was pure. "God . . . breathed into his nostrils the breath of life; and man became a living soul" (Gen. 2:7). God created man in his own image. "And God said, Let us make man in our image, after our likeness. . . . So God created man in his own image, in the image of God created he him" (1:26-27). This image of God was like a coin, having two sides. On the one side, the natural image of God: namely, the intellectual capacity which lifts man above the beasts. "And have put on the new man, which is renewed in knowledge after the image of him that created him" (Col. 3:10). The ancient Jewish rabbis, and some Christian theologians, believed that this natural image included immortality. The other side of this coin was the moral image: "And that ye put on the new man, which after God is created in righteousness and true holiness" (Eph. 4:24). This moral image of God was marred to practical destruction after the fall. Man lost his holiness.

The remaining broken and injured fragments of this image of God we call conscience. It is not, as some say, a separate faculty of the soul, but it is the total consciousness of man—intellect, emotion, and will—working in the area of moral and spiritual realities. Just as a mathematician or an artist cultivates his capacity to see, think, feel, and reason in his particular field, so does the moral nature of man act in its own field by the means and methods appropriate thereto. In other words, conscience is in a way like the capacity of the artist to see, to judge, and to create beauty. Man as God created him was "very good" (Gen. 1:31).

Placed on Probation

The story of the Garden of Eden is so familiar, it needs no elaboration: "And the Lord God planted a garden eastward in Eden; and there he put the man whom he had formed. And out of the ground made the Lord God to grow every tree that is pleasant to the sight, and good for food; the tree of life also in the midst of the garden, and the tree of knowledge of good and evil. . . . And the Lord God took the man and put him into the garden of Eden to dress it and to keep it. And the Lord God commanded the man, saying, Of every tree of the garden thou mayest freely eat; but of the tree of the knowledge of good and evil, thou shalt not eat of it: for in the day that thou eatest thereof thou shalt surely die" (Gen. 2:8-9, 15-17). Then follows the story of how, tempted by Satan, the woman ate and gave to the man, and he did eat. After this they were cast out of Eden and sentenced under a curse.

Skeptics ridicule this story. They scoff at such a heavy penalty for so trivial an act. The reply is that the force of temptation was also light and small. They ate when they were not hungry. Being extremely intelligent, they allowed themselves to be duped by a naive trick. In no heat of passion or pressure of pain they committed treason against their best friend. They put their own wish above the divine law at the very first opportunity. They doubted against virtual knowledge of sight.

Condemned to Death

Many of modern times, yielding to the blandishments of scientific materialism, have asserted that Adam (Man) must have died physically regardless of his obedience, just like the animals.

This position fails to take account of the special condition of man as having an animal-plus nature. That man should die like all other animals is a reasonable conclusion except for the express statement of revelation. Without citing all the evidence we may state the simple conclusion: Man was naturally mortal, but he was given access to the tree of life which would have staved off death day by day, as he ate of it, until at last in the fullness of time he would have walked with God into eternity, as Enoch did without ever tasting death. "Come, ye blessed of my father, inherit the kingdom prepared for you before the foundation of the world" (Matt. 25:34). God threatened man with death, if he disobeyed. After the Fall, God said, "Because thou . . . hast eaten of the tree . . . in the sweat of thy face shalt thou eat bread, till thou return unto the ground; for out of it wast thou taken; for dust thou art, and unto dust shalt thou return" (Gen. 3:17-19).

Death is both spiritual and natural. Spiritual death took effect on man at the instant of his sin, but natural death was postponed by the grace of God. "And the Lord God said, Behold the man is become as one of us to know good and evil:

and now, lest he put forth his hand, and take also of the tree of life, and eat, and live forever: therefore the Lord God sent him forth from the garden of Eden. . . . So he drove out the man" (Gen. 3:22-24).

The resurrection of the body is a part of our redemption: "For since by man came death, by man came also the resurrection of the dead" (I Cor. 15:21).

Universal Human Depravity

Perhaps no doctrine of Scripture is more repugnant to scientific materialism than the teaching of universal human depravity and the consequent necessity of an atonement through Christ. The nineteenth century was a veritable ice age of materialistic skepticism, which resulted in atheistic professors in the university and rationalistic professors in the seminary. But the horrors of two world wars and the marvelous developments of science have weakened materialistic philosophy to the point where millions are willing to hear the voice of Scripture concerning these inscrutable mysteries of human life. This is what the Scriptures teach, and there is not space enough to attempt debate.

When man sinned, he lost the moral image of God. Therefore he could not transmit to his progeny what he did not possess. Men deny that evil could be transmitted in human nature. Although we know that some evil diseases are transmitted through heredity, let us not stop to argue that. The point is that no man can deny that a human being can inherit poverty. A millionaire father loses his money, and all he can transmit to his son is poverty. Furthermore, in many nations, treason on the part of the father visits poverty and many evils on his son however innocent. When Adam lost the image of God, he could no longer transmit that image by heredity to his son. He could only beget "a son in his own likeness, after his image" (Gen. 5:3).

Original Sin Defined

The term "original sin" is not found in the Bible, but it is a common term in theology, and being in the language of universal Christianity, deserves definition. The ninth of the Thirty-Nine Articles of the Church of England (1571) defines original sin as follows: "Of Original or Birth Sin: Original Sin standeth not in the following of Adam (as the Pelagians do vainly talk); but it is the fault and corruption of the Nature of every man, that naturally is engendered of the offspring of Adam; whereby man is very far gone from original righteousness and is of his own Nature inclined to evil. . . ."

Preachers commonly speak of the "Adamic nature," the "carnal nature," and sometimes of the "old man" or "inbred depravity." "Original sin" is a good term, because all theologians know what it means. Some reasons for the belief in original sin may be set forth:

1. The widespread wickedness among the nations. The prevalence of gross idolatry, superstition, war, immorality, and cruelty, and the misery of the masses inflicted by their superiors.

2. The demonic strength of evil passions which override all laws and restraints to commit the foulest crimes.

3. The sources of these blackest vices may be found in the most innocent children and in the most sheltered homes. It is not merely a contagious but an inherited infection.

4. Men find these seeds of evil, each in his own heart.

5. After deciding to be good, one finds the greatest obstacles within himself.

Bible Teaching About Original Sin

When Adam sinned, the penalty was death, spiritual and temporal. Although the gospel makes provision for this penalty, that does not affect the state in which man is born. It is only provisionally available to him, until he definitely accepts (or rejects) it. Therefore man is born in that state of spiritual death which Adam bequeathed to us, because of his lack of the image of God. It is true that the atonement contains the provision for the restoration of the image of God, thus canceling the Fall, but that is conditional upon man's acceptance. Thus Adam begat a son in his own likeness. Noah's flood came because "God saw that the wickedness of man was great in the earth, and that every imagination of the thoughts of his heart was only evil continually" (Gen. 6:5). After the flood God said: "I will not again curse the ground any more for man's sake: for the imagination of man's heart is evil from his youth" (8:21). This indicates hereditary evil in man.

Man is born morally intractable. "Who can bring a clean thing out of an unclean?" (Job 14:4). No man can be born holy. "What is man, that he should be clean? and he which is born of a woman, that he should be righteous? (15:14). "Behold, I was shapen in iniquity, and in sin did my mother conceive me" (Ps. 51:5). "The wicked are estranged from the womb: they go astray as soon as they be born, speaking lies" (Ps. 58:3-4). This teaches inbred depravity. "The rod and reproof give wisdom, but a child left to himself bringeth his mother to shame" (Prov. 29:15).

In Romans 3:10-12, Paul quotes the following passage to prove inbred sin: "The Lord looked down from heaven upon the children of men, to see if there were any that did understand, and seek God. They are all gone aside, they are all together become filthy: there is none that doeth good, no, not one" (Ps. 14:2-3). Jesus said, "From within, out of the heart of men, proceed evil thoughts, adulteries, . . . murders: . . . all these things come from within, and defile the man" (Mark 7:21-23). "Madness is in their heart while they live" (Eccles. 9:3). "Ye being evil know how to give good gifts unto your children" (Matt. 7:11). "Thou savorest not the things that be of God; but the things that be of men" (Matt. 16:23). "Are ye not carnal, and walk as men?" (I Cor. 3:3). "That he no longer should live the rest of his time in the flesh to the lusts of men, but to the will of God" (I Pet. 4:2). "We are of God and the whole world lieth in wickedness" (I John 5:19). "That ye put off . . . the old man" (Eph. 4:22).

The necessity of a new birth would seem to indicate something radically wrong with man. "Except a man be born of water and of the Spirit, he cannot enter into the kingdom of God. That which is born of the flesh is flesh; and that which is born of the Spirit is spirit" (John 3:5-6). Some thought is necessary here to grasp our Lord's meaning that all persons born of natural flesh have a sinful nature. The New Testament teaches that it is the spirit of man which defiles his flesh, not the contrary. Nevertheless, the New Testament often uses the term "flesh" to designate the sinful or carnal nature of man. For example: "I know that in me (that is, in my flesh,) dwelleth no good thing" (Rom. 7:18). "There is therefore now no condemnation to them which are in Christ Jesus, who walk not after the flesh, but after the Spirit. . . . They that are after the flesh do mind the things of the flesh; but they that are after the Spirit the things of the Spirit. So then they that are in the flesh cannot please God. But ye are not in the flesh, but in the Spirit" (8:1, 5, 8-9).

Proof that the "flesh" here does not mean the human body is given by the assertion, "Ye are not in the flesh." Yet these people were living human beings. They were not in the flesh of the old sinful nature because they were living the life of the Spirit of God. Combining the evidence of these texts then, we learn that children born of natural birth partake of the nature of the flesh of sin, in which state they cannot please God, and must be born again.

Run quickly down Romans 3. Both Jews and Gentiles are all under sin, "For all have sinned, and come short of the glory of God." Here we have universal terms "all," "every," "all the world," "both Jews and Gentiles." The language of Paul traces all sin to Adam. "Wherefore, as by one man sin entered into the world, and death by sin; and so death passed upon all men, for that all have sinned" (5:12). For Paul, the fact of death is the proof of sin. True, infants who are personally innocent, die; but their death is one of the consequences of Adam's sin. Many theologians have said that death is the penalty of Adam's sin, and that the child is guilty of Adam's sin. Some of them use the term "guilt" in an impersonal way. But we prefer to call death the consequence of Adam's sin. One should follow this argument through the rest of the chapter. This theme is taken up again in I Cor. 15:22: "For as in Adam all die, even so in Christ shall all be made alive."

How Man Inherits Moral Depravity

Some skeptics have accused the orthodox of saying that God himself has injected some foul infection of evil into the innocent souls of unborn children. However, we only say that original sin is not something infused into innocent children. It is the result of the deprivation of human nature of the moral image of God. Moreover positive evil results from this loss, just as rickets results from the loss of lime in the bones. Without the lime the bones become weak and deformed. And without the image of God, man's nature bends under the weight of temptation. It becomes morally deformed; that is, depraved. The image of God includes an emotional urge to do right. We do not say this urge is destroyed, but it is bent and deformed. The man's heart is depraved.

We inherit depravity just as a man inherits poverty. Our parents did not possess the image of God; therefore they could not give it to us. The question of the origin of the soul is generally supposed to enter in here. We believe, as before stated, that the soul comes to us from our ancestors, just as our body does. But the point is not determinant for the inheritance of original sin. However man receives his soul, his humanity he receives from his parents. The result is always the same.

Some have argued that if both parents should have the

image of God restored, as in entire sanctification, then their children should inherit the image of God. Here the answer is plain: The restoration of the image of God is entirely a personal gift—like the office of President of the United States. It can be enjoyed fully, but it cannot be inherited.

Chapter IV

CHRIST, THE ATONEMENT FOR SIN

HISTORICAL THEORIES OF THE ATONEMENT

An early theory declares that Christ's atonement was a ransom paid to the devil. The New Testament teaches that Christ was a ransom for us. But to whom was this ransom paid? Gregory of Nyssa (331-395) taught that men had sold themselves into slavery to the devil, and that Christ, disguised by his humanity, surrendered himself into the hands of the devil as men's ransom. However, when Christ's deity became manifest the devil found himself unable to hold either Christ or men. In modern times Bishop Aulen of Sweden has found a grain of value in this theory, despite its crudity.

Perhaps the greatest theory in point of historic interest is that of Anselm (1033-1109) who elaborated the satisfaction theory, emphasizing the merit of Christ's work which is transferred to men, or placed to their account, and offsets the demands of divine justice.

The moral influence theory is the doctrine that the death of Christ never had any legal or technical value as being in any wise analogous to a legal or commercial contract. Its entire effectiveness depended upon the moral influence which it exerted upon the hearts of men to soften and refine them and to lead them to repentance. This is a favorite doctrine with Unitarians and other liberals. Although there is some truth in it, it is far from the whole truth.

The governmental theory is the doctrine that the standards of God's moral government must be sustained for the moral welfare of mankind. In its revolt against what it considers the harshness and legalism of the substitutionary doctrine of

75

atonement, it regards the sacrifice of Christ as an expedient whereby the honor and majesty of moral government are sustained in connection with the offer of pardon to the sinner. The doctrine was formulated by Grotius (1583-1645). It has had the support of many prominent Methodist theologians and a wide popularity among their ministers. It leans too far toward liberalism; although it was held in modified form by such conservatives as Richard Watson.

Doubtless the principal weakness with each of the foregoing theories and of many others, is not what they contain, so much as what they leave out. We believe the truth is only to be found in the revelation of God, and we doubt the power of philosophy to understand and expound every phase of that truth adequately. For us, the substitutionary theory grasps an essential element in New Testament teaching, but we have little confidence either in the philosophical arguments which support it or in the philosophical arguments which have tended to make it ridiculous in much modern theological literature. We believe that Christ tasted death for every man in a sense above the range of philosophy to justify or deny.

CHRIST IS MEDIATOR

The One who makes atonement for sin is the Mediator who stands between God and man, partaking of both natures. Elsewhere we have studied passages attesting the deity of Christ. Christ's humanity is also treated elsewhere. We merely call attention to it here.

Christ Is the God-Man

This is the place to emphasize the Scripture passages which show Christ as the divine-human Mediator. He is "made of the seed of David according to the flesh; and declared to be the Son of God with power" (Rom. 1:3-4). In Hebrews 9:14 Christ's divinity is implied: "The blood of Christ, who through the eternal spirit offered himself without spot to God, purge your conscience." Peter notes that Christ was "put to death in the flesh, but quickened by the Spirit" (I Pet. 3:18). The divine-human nature of Christ is mentioned by Paul. He refers to the Israelites "of whom as concerning the flesh Christ came, who is over all, God blessed forever" (Rom. 9:5). "God was manifest in the flesh, justified in the Spirit" (I Tim. 3:16). This Mediator is Christ Jesus, "who, being in the form of God, thought it not robbery to be equal with God: but made himself of no reputation, and took upon him the form of a servant, and was made in the likeness of men" (Phil. 2:6-7). God sent "his own son in the likeness of sinful flesh" (Rom. 8:3). "And the Word became flesh, and dwelt among us" (John 1:14). This Man after he had offered one sacrifice for sins forever sat down on the right hand of God. "What and if ye shall see the Son of man ascend up where he was before?" (6:62). "I came forth from the Father, and am come into the world: again I leave the world, and go to the Father" (16:28). "Your father Abraham rejoiced to see my day. . . . Before Abraham was, I am" (8:56-58). "Who is he that condemneth? It is Christ that died, yea rather, that is risen again, who is even at the right hand of God, who also maketh intercession for us." Here the deity and manhood of Christ and his mediatorial work are set forth.

Christ's Atonement Typified

Old Testament sacrifices typify Christ's atonement. "If any one of the common people sin, . . . he shall bring his offering . . . for his sin which he hath sinned . . . and the priest shall burn it upon the altar . . . and the priest shall make an atonement for him, and it shall be forgiven him" (Lev. 4:27-31). The offering is typical of Christ who is sacrificed for us. "Behold the Lamb of God, which taketh away the sin of the world" (John 1:29).

Likewise, the priest typifies Christ. "This man, because he continueth ever, hath an unchangeable priesthood" (Heb. 7:24). "And he shall take of the congregation of the children of Israel two kids of the goats for a sin offering. . . . And Aaron shall bring the goat . . . and offer him for a sin offering. But the goat, on which the lot fell to be the scapegoat . . . let him go for a scapegoat into the wilderness. . . . And Aaron shall lay both his hands on the head of the live goat, and confess over him all the iniquities of the children of Israel, and all their transgressions in all their sins, putting them upon the head of the goat, and shall send him away . . . and the goat shall bear upon him all their iniquities unto a land not inhabited" (Lev. 16:5-22).

This marvelous passage evinces a superhuman ingenuity in symbolizing the two natures of Christ (God and man) by two goats—one killed, and another who never died but bore away man's iniquities. The slain goat typifies the man Christ Jesus who died for our sins according to the Scriptures. The other goat is (on the record) deathless. He symbolizes Christ resurrected; also the God nature that could not die.

The Need of Atonement

The law of God is universal. The penalty of its violation is death. All have sinned and come short of the glory of God. Without a miracle, people once dead are forever dead. Without the shedding of blood there is no remission for sin. "If there had been a law given which could have given life, verily righteousness should have been by the law. But the scripture hath concluded all under sin, that the promise by faith of Jesus Christ might be given to them that believe" (Gal. 3:21-22). There is no provision in the law for salvation—that can come alone by grace, through the atonement of Christ.

The idea that God can hate sin and love the sinner is anathema to our generation. Yet if an innocent child is kidnaped and cruelly murdered simply for money, the public is wrathful. Likewise, they are wroth when their own kind are murdered as helpless prisoners of war. Hence it is easy to see that the unspoiled conscience of unprejudiced men is able to sense the mysterious and eternally just wrath of God against whatever is really evil (and God's vision is keener than ours).

Repentance of itself cannot save man from the penalty of his sins. First, repentance cannot restore the broken law of holiness; it cannot pay the debt of the pauper. Even if it could do so, repentance itself is only possible by the influence of the Holy Spirit, forfeited by sin. Our only hope is Christ "in whom we have redemption through his blood, the forgiveness of sins" (Eph. 1:7). "The Son of man came . . . to give his life a ransom for many" (Matt. 20:28). "Who gave himself a ransom for all" (I Tim. 2:6). "Behold the Lamb of God, which taketh away the sin of the world" (John 1:29). "And the bread that I will give is my flesh, which I will give for the life of the world." Then he adds, "Except ye eat the flesh of the Son of man and drink his blood, ye have no life in you" (6:51-53). Here salvation is denied to any who receive it not through Christ's death.

"Much more then, being justified by his blood, we shall be saved from wrath through him" (Rom. 5:9). "In whom we have redemption through his blood, even the forgiveness of sins" (Col. 1:14). "Ye were not redeemed with corruptible things, as silver and gold . . . but with the precious blood of Christ, as of a lamb without blemish and without spot" (I Pet. 1:18-19). "But if we walk in the light, as he is in the light, we have fellowship one with another, and the blood of Jesus Christ his son cleanseth us from all sin" (I John 1:7). "Unto him that loved us, and washed us from our sins in his own blood" (Rev. 1:5). "Thou wast slain, and hast redeemed us to God by thy blood" (5:9). And have washed their robes and made them white in the blood of the Lamb" (7:14). "He was wounded for our transgressions. He bare the sin of many" (Isa. 53:5-12). "Who was delivered for our offenses, and raised again for our justification" (Rom. 4:25). "Christ died for our sins according to the scriptures" (I Cor. 15:3). "Who his own self bare our sins in his own body on the tree" (I Pet. 2:24). "For Christ also hath once suffered for sins, the just for the unjust, that he might bring us to God" (3:18). "So Christ was once offered to bear the sin of many (Heb. 9:28). "But we see Jesus, who was made a little lower than the angels for the suffering of death, crowned with glory and honor; that he by the grace of God should taste death for every man" (2:9).

We have omitted comment only for the lack of space, although we are fully aware of the contempt which some scholars have for this method. We honestly believe that plain Scripture texts will be more valuable than philosophical comment. They prove that Christ "is the propitiation for our sins: and not for ours only, but also for the sins of the whole world" (I John 2:2). "Neither by the blood of goats and calves, but by his own blood he entered in once into the holy place, having obtained eternal redemption for us. For if the blood of bulls and of goats, and the ashes of an heifer sprinkling the unclean, sanctifieth to the purifying of the flesh: how much more shall the blood of Christ, who through the eternal spirit offered himself without spot to God, purge your conscience? . . . And for this cause he is the mediator of the new testament" (Heb. 9:12-15).

Chapter V

JESUS, THE SAVIOR FROM SIN

"Thou shalt call his name Jesus, for he shall save his people from their sins" (Matt. 1:21).

Salvation and Predestination

God's Calling and Election

Major Calvinistic works devote vast space to the doctrines of the calling and the election of believers. Because these are treated from a predestinarian standpoint, Arminian theologians sometimes omit the discussion at this point. While we cannot believe with Calvinists that God has from all eternity predestinated some to be damned irretrievably and others elected to be saved unconditionally, we do believe that there is a calling from God to all men to salvation; for he is "not willing that any should perish, but that all should come to repentance" (II Pet. 3:9).

God called and elected the nation of Israel to be his people. Undoubtedly, as the record shows, millions of them rejected that calling, and only a small remnant were saved. The church is the new Israel. All its members were called and elected in the same way, but many men have rejected the call, and some even despised the election after they were saved. Jesus said in his prayer: "Those that thou gavest me [the elect] I have kept, and none of them is lost, but the son of perdition [Judas]; that the scripture might be fulfilled" (John 17:12). Here, plainly, one of the elect was lost.

Undoubtedly God has predestinated every man and called every man to be saved. But some resist. "And they that resist shall receive to themselves damnation" (Rom. 13:2). Peter calls the church, "elect according to the foreknowledge of God the Father." As we have elsewhere shown, the term "to know" in the Bible often means to regard favorably. Thus at the great judgment Christ says to the lost: "I know you not whence ye are; depart . . ." (Luke 13: 27). Of course, it is blasphemy to say that Christ was actually ignorant of these people. He did not know them in the sense of being gracious to them, for the day of grace was past.

Our God is not a cold, heartless machine. It is comforting to know that he foreknew us, that he held us in gracious esteem before we were born. He predestined us and called us and elected us to grace and love before we were born, just as many a parent has done his child. "Wherefore the rather, brethren, give diligence to make your calling and election sure, for if ye do these things ye shall never fall" (II Pet. 1: 10).

God's Love and Predestination

The Bible is so full of assertions repeated over and over again concerning God's love for all men and desire that all men may be saved that it would not only be laborious to copy them all out here, it would swell the size of this book beyond its possible limits. The total of these texts is staggering and their meaning beyond debate. This fact has baffled many students in view of the few texts which seem to teach predestination.

Doubtless the origin of the Scriptures in Hebrew, Chaldee, and Greek has given room for the misinterpretation of a few words on which the debate turns. We Arminians believe that such terms as predestinate, foreknow, call, elect, simply indicate God's purpose for his creatures which can be overruled by them in stubbornness and rebellion. Thus foreknowledge is the kindly thought of God for us before we were born; predestination simply means that, like a good parent, God has a plan for our life, if we will follow it. Calling and election mean that God has a place for us in his church and kingdom, if we do not reject it. Many parents have planned like that (sometimes futilely) for their children.

The Potter and the Clay

Probably the strongest argument for the fatalistic view of predestination (remember, we believe in nonfatalistic predestination) is founded on the potter passage in Jeremiah. "Then I went down to the potter's house, and, behold, he wrought a work on the wheels. And the vessel that he made of clay was marred in the hand of the potter: so he made it again another vessel, as seemed good to the potter to make it" (18: 3-4).

As we contemplate this historic text upon which such a massive structure has been built, we may well be staggered by the enormity of the misconceptions about it. A child should be able to see that the first thing the parable teaches is the failure and disappointment of the potter. I grant that this is not a philosophical concept of God. But it is a normal Hebrew concept, and the kind of thing which abounds in the Bible. Theologians call these forms of speech anthropomorphisms (human figures of speech applied to God). Some famous theologians of our time believe that the God of the philosophers is simply different from the God of the Bible.

Anyhow, this parable teaches that the potter tried to make a good vessel, but he failed, owing to some flaw in the material. This certainly does not teach that God plans to ruin any man. God seeks to make each man a vessel unto honor. Why the failure? Because of some flaw in the clay. How could that be true in any human life, except by a flaw of rebellion and disobedience in the human being here represented by the vessel? How could God fail in his plans? Because he has limited himself intentionally and with full knowledge by creating man with freedom of will.

This parable further teaches that the work of the Potter is not finished before life begins. Quite the contrary! The whirling earth is the turning wheel of the Potter, measuring out the time of man's earthly life. And the hands of the Potter are the forces of divine providence shaping the circumstances of our earthly career. Notice further that the Potter tried again. Even though he had failed, he made the best vessel still possible. How absurd to call such trial and failure and repeated trials, in which a potter makes something different from what he intended at first, by the name of predestination!

REDEMPTION IN CHRIST

Many Phases of Redemption

It is customary and quite proper for Christians to speak of the beginning of their Christian life as one event, and such it is. But theologians commonly divide the experience into its component parts. At the beginning of the Christian life a person becomes justified, converted, regenerated, born again, and adopted. This all happens at once and to the same person, just as the President when elected is made at once head of the Army, of the Navy, and of the Air Force, tenant of the White House, and President of the United States.

The term "justification" does not describe all that happens to a new convert. It is a term from the law court and indicates what God does outside the man on the divine record books. Justification indicates that a man has been released from God's awful bar of justice as no longer guilty of the sins and crimes formerly held against him; he is forgiven utterly and completely. He is no longer amenable to punishment. He is forgiven on the ground of the atonement of Christ.

The Conditions of Justification

Faith is the essential condition of justification. "Abraham believed God, and it was counted unto him for righteousness" (Rom. 4:3). Righteousness, here, is the legal state of a forgiven man. The faith necessary includes assent to the truth, but it is principally trust in the promise that "the blood of Jesus Christ his Son cleanseth us from all sin" (I John 1:7).

The first recorded preaching of Christ was "Repent ye, and

believe the gospel" (Mark 1:15). It has long been debated whether salvation may be preached as by faith alone, or by repentance and faith, but following Paul and the great Arminian theologians we say, Salvation is by faith alone. Although one cannot exercise saving faith till after he repents, nevertheless the order is not without importance. To posit salvation on faith and repentance is to join repentance, which is a work, to faith, which is the renunciation of all works, as a means of salvation. One must repent before he can believe, but here the road is very narrow, and faith is the only companion. The traveler is one who has repented and who now believes.

Repentance is much more than many persons understand. It involves a deep revulsion from, a sincere distaste of, and a real sorrow for, every possible sin in general and his own personal sins in particular. True penitence leads one to forsake his sins and amend his life, and the best way one can tell whether he is sorry enough for his sins is to forsake them. The person who is only sorry he has been caught has no true repentance but the sorrow of the world that "worketh death" (II Cor. 7:10).

Repentance is a gift from God. "Then hath God also to the Gentiles granted repentance unto life" (Acts 11:18). It comes through the conviction of the Holy Spirit "who when he is come will reprove the world of sin" (John 16:8). Likewise faith is a gift of God: "For unto you it is given . . . to believe on him" (Phil. 1:29). This is all a result of what is called the prevenient grace of God; that is, the grace granted in mercy to sinners to make it possible for them to turn from sin to God. This means that any sinner could be convicted and saved anywhere, if only he would give as much attention to his soul's salvation as he would to buying a car.

Children of God by Regeneration

Regeneration is the experience when we are "born again . . . not of blood, nor of the will of the flesh, nor of the will of man, but of God" (John 3:3; 1:13). "A new heart also will I give you, and a new spirit will I put within you: and I will take away the stony heart out of your flesh, and I will give you an heart of flesh. And I will put my Spirit within you, and cause you to walk in my statutes" (Ezek. 36:26-27). Old things pass away; all things become new (II Cor. 5:17). The Christian is a new man (Eph. 4:22-24; Col. 3:9-10; I John 3:9; 4:7; 5:4; Rom. 8:2-4).

Sonship is an inevitable consequence of being born of God. "As many as received him, to them gave he power to become the sons of God, even to them that believe on his name" (John 1:12).

Adoption is another term for regeneration. "That ye might receive the adoption of sons. And because ye are sons, God hath sent forth the Spirit of his Son into your hearts, crying, Abba, Father" (Gal. 4:5).

We must remember that there is not even an infinitely small measure of time between justification and regeneration. Each is only a separate logical aspect of one crisis of salvation. Conversion is the popular term for the human side of the experience of regeneration.

"Ye have not received the spirit of bondage again to fear; but ye have received the Spirit of adoption, whereby we cry, Abba, Father. The Spirit himself beareth witness with our spirit, that we are the children of God" (Rom. 8:15-16). "In whom also after that ye believed, ye were sealed with that Holy Spirit of promise, which is the earnest of our inheritance until the redemption of the purchased possession" (Eph. 1:13-14). These scriptures teach that the believer is entitled to an assurance of salvation. The witness of the Spirit of God is accompanied by the witness of a good conscience. The practical rule is given by John: "For if our heart condemn us, God is greater than our heart, and knoweth all things. Beloved, if our heart condemn us not, then have we confidence toward God" (I John 3:20-21).

What Do the Regenerate Lack?

After Isaac blessed Jacob (Gen. 27) he was baffled upon the return of Esau to find a blessing for him, as it seemed he had given all to Jacob. Upon reflection, however, he found a blessing for Esau. In like manner, theologians for ages have been baffled to find what further blessings can appertain to entire sanctification than have already been received in regeneration. In regeneration the man is born again, washed from his sins, made a new man in Christ Jesus. The scriptures add up to a long list of ineffable blessings. The soul who has received this abounding grace might well ask: "What lack I yet?"

Nevertheless, every evangelical creed written before the nineteenth century specifically stipulated that remains of original sin continued in the regenerate. And this we accept and believe.

How can these things be in such a man as the regenerate? By turning to our explanation of depravity by deprivation, we may find an answer to our question. The regenerate is a babe in Christ. "And I brethren could not speak to you as unto spiritual, but as unto carnal, even as unto babes in Christ" (I Cor. 3:1). See also I Peter 2:1-2. We have defined the cause of original sin as a defect, a lack of the image of God. The remaining original sin in the regenerate is simply this lack of manhood in the babes in Christ. Nor does the explanation that the maturity of manhood is gained by growth suffice, for these are only metaphors—parables which must not be applied literally in every particular. But even if we unnecessarily follow the parable literally, we need not miss the scriptural truth. Manhood is a gift. This is proved by the fact that some do not receive it by growth. It is an addition to the normal life of children. The Scriptures teach that spiritual maturity is a gift which must be sought in grace, and not in growth. The following text properly interpreted so teaches: "And he gave some apostles; and some, prophets; and some, evangelists; and some, pastors and teachers; for the perfecting of the saints, for the work of the ministry, for the edifying of the body of Christ: till we all come in the unity of the faith, and of the knowledge of the Son of God, unto a perfect man, unto the measure of the stature of the fullness of Christ" (Eph. 4:11-13). Here the perfecting of the saints brings them to the fullness of Christ, to the perfect manhood of the Master. "Edifying," nowadays, often means "entertaining." Here it means building up the church which is only done by evangelistic effort. The whole emphasis here is not on natural growth but upon evangelism and spiritual work.

THE DOCTRINE OF ETERNAL SECURITY

The doctrine now widely preached under the title of "eternal security" was formerly preached in this country as "the final perseverance of the saints." It teaches that a truly regenerate person can never be finally lost. As final perseverance, it usually held that the believer who fell into sin, would be followed by the grace of God, and recovered before his death. Eternal security advocates teach that no sin which a saved man can ever commit will be sufficient to damn him. The doctrine comes down to us from Calvinism, although it appears that the peculiar development it has undergone in passing from the final perseverance to eternal security is the result of the influence of the Plymouth Brethren.

Security Is Conditional

The Bible teaches only a conditional security. "If ye do these things ye shall never fall" (II Pet. 1:10). The Bible teaches plainly that the only way to keep from falling is to avoid sinning; for to sin is to fall. No one ever fell from God except through sin, and no one ever sinned without falling. "Solomon, my son, know thou the God of thy father: . . . if thou seek him, he will be found of thee; but if thou forsake him he will cast thee off forever" (I Chron. 28:9). The Scriptures plainly teach that the righteous may fall away into sin, and be lost forever. "But when the righteous turneth away from his righteousness and doeth iniquity, and doeth according to all the abominations that the wicked man doeth, shall he live?" Here the eternal security teachers will answer, "Yes, undoubtedly." But the Scriptures continue, "All his righteousness that he hath done shall not be mentioned: in his trespass that he hath trespassed, and in his sin that he hath sinned, in them shall he die" (Ezek. 18:24).

The Christian's righteousness is not self-righteousness. It is a righteousness which would save him—if he continued in it: "In his righteousness that he hath done shall he live" (vs. 22). Again we read: "When I shall say to the righteous that he shall surely live; if he trust to his own righteousness, and commit iniquity, all his righteousnesses shall not be remembered; but for his iniquity that he hath committed, he shall die for it" (33:13).

"Abide in me, and I in you. As the branch cannot bear fruit of itself, except it abide in the vine; no more can ye, except ye abide in me. I am the vine, ye are the branches: he that abideth in me, and I in him, the same bringeth forth much fruit: for without me ye can do nothing." That this exhortation to abide shows the possibility of falling is shown by the following verse: "If a man abide not in me, he is cast forth as a branch, and is withered" (John 15:4-6). Each of these branches was equally as secure as the others, but some were "cast forth, and burned" because they were unfruitful. They are hopelessly lost forever.

Christians may fall from grace. "Christ is become of no effect unto you, whosoever of you are justified by the law; ye are fallen from grace" (Gal. 5:4).

The Book of Hebrews was written to Christians under pressure to forsake Christianity and return to Judaism in order to escape persecution. The writer warns them (chaps. 6 and

10) that such an apostasy from Christ will ruin their hopes of heaven forever. Peter warns of the danger of apostasy from Christ. "But he that lacketh these things is blind, and cannot see afar off, and hath forgotten that he was purged from his old sins. Wherefore the rather, brethren, give diligence to make your calling and election sure: for if ye do these things, ye shall never fall" (II Pet. 1: 9-10). No careful man can question that the persons of verse 9 were apostates, for they had been purged from their old sins. "For if after they have escaped the pollutions of the world through the knowledge of the Lord and Savior Jesus Christ, they are again entangled therein, and overcome, the latter end is worse with them than the beginning. For it had been better for them not to have known the way of righteousness, than, after they have known it, to turn from the holy commandment delivered unto them" (2: 20-21). This passage really requires no interpretation. It only needs to be taken seriously. The man who plays with this solemn text, and sins willfully under pretext of being morally infallible deliberately deceives and damns his own soul.

Examples of Final Apostasy

Some of the angels sinned and fell forever. "God spared not the angels that sinned, but cast them down to hell, and delivered them into chains of darkness, to be reserved unto judgment" (II Pet. 2: 4). Eve, the mother of all living, was created holy, without sin, but she fell into sin. The Apostle Paul warned the Corinthian brethren against apostasy by her example: "But I fear, lest by any means, as the serpent beguiled Eve through his subtlety, so your minds should be corrupted from the simplicity that is in Christ" (II Cor. 11: 3). Here is proof positive that Paul did not believe in eternal security. The children of Israel who came out of Egypt were all godly as described by Paul. "And were all baptized unto Moses in the cloud and in the sea; and did all eat the same spiritual meat, and did all drink the same spiritual drink." Nevertheless these saints fell, for continuing he says, "But with many of them God was not well pleased: for they were overthrown in the wilderness. . . . Wherefore let him that thinketh he standeth take heed lest he fall" (I Cor. 10:2-12).

Here the Apostle shows that although they were all partakers of the spiritual meat and drink of Christ, nevertheless many of them fell into sin and apostasy and died lost. King Saul fell. "And the Spirit of the Lord will come upon thee, and thou shalt prophesy with them, and shalt be turned into another man" (I Sam. 10:6). And yet this same man apostatized and went into hopeless sin against God. Then it was that "the Spirit of the Lord departed from Saul" (16:14). Why did it depart? "Thou hast rejected the word of the Lord, and he hath rejected thee from being king" (15:26).

King Solomon was greatly honored of God, but he fell. "For it came to pass, when Solomon was old, that his wives turned away his heart after other gods" (I Kings 11:4). An apostle fell. Here was a man, who "was numbered with us, and had obtained part of this ministry." Those who say Judas was never saved deny flatly the Word of God. In praying over the election of a successor to Judas the apostles petitioned: "That he may take part of this ministry and apostleship, from which Judas by transgression fell (Acts 1:17, 25). Some of Paul's helpers fell. "Holding faith, and a good conscience; which some having put away concerning faith have made shipwreck: of whom in Hymeneus and Alexander" (I Tim. 1:19-20). "Nevertheless, I have somewhat against thee, because thou hast left thy first love. Remember therefore from whence thou art fallen, and repent" (Rev. 2:4-5).

To sin is to fall: "He that committeth sin is of the devil. . . . Whosoever is born of God doth not commit sin. . . . In this the children of God are manifest, and the children of the devil" (I John 3:8-10). "Brethren, if any of you do err from the truth, and one convert him; let him know that he which converteth the sinner from the error of his way shall save a soul from death, and shall hide a multitude of sins" (Jas. 5:19-20). "If any man see his brother sin a sin which is not unto death [not the unpardonable sin], he shall ask, and he shall give him life for them that sin not unto death. There is a sin unto death [possible for a brother]: I do not say that he shall pray for it" (I John 5:16). This is an exhortation to pray for backsliders and apostates.

Chapter VI

CHRIST, THE SANCTIFIER

THE MEANING OF THE HOLY

The subject of this discussion is lightly held by many Christians and regarded with indifference by others, largely because they have no comprehension of its meaning. Perhaps the majority of Christians regard any pretensions to holiness as nothing less than brazen hypocrisy. Persons meddling with the subject are presumed to be abysmally ignorant and doubtless mentally deranged. This is strange in view of the habitual religious tolerance of Americans and of the fact that the doctrine of entire sanctification in its modern form originated with the Friends and the Methodists—two denominations highly regarded in our country.

Sanctification and holiness both mean the same thing, as "sanctification" comes from the Latin word *sanctus*, which means "holy." One is amazed that devout Christians should abhor the word holy, for its primary meaning is simply "the thing which belongs to God." Scan a concordance and you find "holy ground," "holy gift," "holy garment," "holy thing," "holy crown," "holy anointing oil," and "a holy people," meaning the Israelites, not as an indication of their superlative goodness, but as a designation of them as a special people who belonged to God as a nation.

Holy and Most Holy

At this point there appears a paradoxical element in the idea of holiness which is likewise represented in the conception of private property. If "holy" means "belonging to God," how can one thing be more holy than another? Yet we make the

93

same practical distinction in regard to property. On a million-aire's estate we regard his watch, purse, and diary, as his private personal possessions, and as such more privileged than a stick or stone on his estate. This is the meaning of the text "a peculiar people" (Titus 2:14), and explains the difference between the "holy" and "most holy" as applied to rooms in the temple. It also explains how, though all Christians are holy from the moment of their conversion, yet only fully consecrated believers possess "entire sanctification."

As long as only *things* belonged to God—such things as sacrifices, pots, pans, and vessels of the altar, the furniture of the temple—it was natural that no moral character was attributed to them. This kind of holiness is called ceremonial holiness, and we find it still mentioned in the New Testament: "The temple sanctifies the gold and the altar sanctifies the gift (Matt. 23:17, 19). "The unbelieving husband is sanctified by the wife, and ... your children ... are ... holy" (I Cor. 7:13).

Whence Moral Purity?

But in course of time persons, such as priests, were attached to the temple, and belonged to the Lord; and it was felt that persons who belonged to God ought to be like God in character. A good slave obeyed his master. The priests were the slaves of God and in duty bound to obey him and do his will. Thus belonging to God was seen to involve moral purity, i.e., moral obedience to God and moral likeness to God. We admit that this is the spiritual meaning of the word, but we insist that we must understand its primary meaning to grasp the subject fully.

The term G.I. has had a similar development in the United States Army patois. For nearly 150 years soldiers wore clothes and used goods marked G.I., meaning "Government Issue"— goods belonging to the government. Then, all at once, they woke up to the fact that they themselves—in a manner—belonged to the government also. So they called themselves G.I. —i.e., government-owned. That is the primary meaning of holy: God-owned. Most writers say that holy means separated —but they omit to state that the reason the holy is separated is because it belongs to God.

The Doctrine of Sanctification

From the beginning of Protestantism in the sixteenth century until the end of the eighteenth century, every evangelical denomination in the world taught that regeneration does not complete the work of sanctification, but that there are remains of original sin left in the regenerate. Most theologians believed these elements of carnality were to be struggled against throughout the whole Christian life. The dominant theory of both Reformed and Lutheran theology is that sanctification is a gradual process of overcoming the carnal nature and subduing it by growth in grace and stern resistance to its inward evil power; and although some will become much better than others, no Christian at his best will ever become entirely free from all sinful tendencies until at the moment of death he becomes entirely sanctified.

Opposed to this is the Wesleyan doctrine—taught by John and Charles Wesley—that the justified believer may consecrate himself fully to God and receive in this life full deliverance from the remains of original sin in his nature by one definite act of faith and one immediate work of grace. This experience has been variously called, entire sanctification, the second blessing, the second work of grace, Christian perfection. We call it the second crisis in redemption. The groups that teach this doctrine are called collectively, the Holiness Movement.

A Need Beyond Regeneration

Logically, at this point the whole argument seems to turn upon the question of whether regeneration is fully adequate. We have taught that the regenerate are saved, born of God, babes in Christ, have a new heart and a new nature, and are born again. Such a person might well ask, "What lack I yet?"

Regeneration is the work of God, and the answer of any pious person must always be that the work of regeneration is adequate for what God intended to do at the time. But this is far from saying that no more than one crisis in redemption is possible.

It cannot be overemphasized that before the days of Wesley every evangelical church in the world taught that there were remains of carnality in the believer. One of the Thirty-Nine Articles of the Church of England reads: "And this infection of nature [original sin] doth remain, yea in them that are regenerated." There is a similar sentence in the law of the Protestant Episcopal Church in the United States. The Lutheran Formula of Concord (1576) speaks of the merely formal obedience of the worldly, and adds, "As also the regenerate do, so far as they are yet carnal," and so for the French Confession of Faith (1559) and the Synod of Dort of the Reformed Church of Holland (1619). The Westminster Confession (1647), foundation creed for all Presbyterianism, says: "This sanctification is throughout the whole man; yet imperfect in this life; there abideth still some remnants of corruption —in every part, whence ariseth a continual and irreconcilable war, the flesh lusting against the spirit, and the spirit against the flesh."

Even the Roman Catholic Church, in the Decrees of the Council of Trent, voices the same belief. "This Holy Synod confesses and is sensible, that in the baptized there remaineth concupiscence, or an incentive to sin. . . . This concupiscence, which the Apostle sometimes calls sin [here the reference is to Romans 6:12; 7:8], the Holy Synod declares that the Catholic Church has never understood it to be sin, as being truly and properly sin in those born again, but because it is of sin and inclines to sin." (See my *Meaning of Sanctification*.) If the Apostle calls this remaining depravity in believers by the name of sin, we do not hesitate to follow him. Here we can add the Roman Catholic Church to the list of those who taught before Wesley that regeneration does not complete the work of sanctification. Some element of carnality remains in the regenerate. So far as I know this unanimous testimony to the doctrine of the remains of sin in believers by all the ancient Christian creeds has not been noted before, but it deserves very heavy emphasis. Ancient Christians agreed on this doctrine more unanimously than on any other, save possibly the deity of Christ. This ought to receive consideration.

Inheritance of the Carnal Nature

It is sometimes used as an argument against entire sanctification that if it were really true, the children of sanctified parents would not inherit the carnal nature. The first thing to say about this is that almost all of our spiritual truths are conveyed by figures of speech which may break down if we make unfair demands of them. Generally the spiritual reality may be regarded as an inscrutable mystery, dimly revealed in a human figure of speech. However, in the case of entire sanctification we have at hand illustrations which clear up this paradox. A millionaire can transmit wealth as an individual personal inheritance to his son. But in America a privileged person cannot transmit his privilege by inheritance. Thus the son of a Rockefeller may inherit the solid wealth of his father, but the son of the President cannot inherit one iota of his father's privileges; for a president does not own the presidency individually; it is a gift from the American people. It goes by grace, not by natural inheritance. Entire sanctification is a privilege which cannot be inherited.

Conditional Justification of Infants

"We see Jesus, who was made a little lower than the angels for the suffering of death, crowned with glory and honor; that he by the grace of God should taste death for every man" (Heb. 2:9). "Therefore as by the offense of one judgment came upon all men to condemnation; even so by the righteousness of one the free gift came upon all men unto justification of life" (Rom. 5:18). Skeptics scoff at the terrible penalties of

Adam's fall. All such should remember that Christ's ranson has conditionally canceled all of Adam's fall. Christ vouched for the safety of infants: "Except ye be converted, and become as little children, ye shall not enter into the kingdom of heaven" (Matt. 18:3).

There seems to be a paradox involved here. All children are saved, and all men are sinners. What is the solution of this difficulty? Simply this: All infants are conditionally justified under the atonement, and their justification stands to their credit until they reject it. If they die before reaching the age of accountability the benefits of the atonement, including regeneration, justification, and entire sanctification, fall to them as the gift of the grace of God. This does not mean that children are saved, regenerated, and justified in the full sense which adult believers enjoy. Neither are they wholly sanctified on account of their passive innocence. If they live, they must actively accept these gifts of the grace of God.

Their state is very much like a citizen's infant child under American law. This child owes hundreds of dollars on the national debt. He never borrowed the money, but he owes it —conditionally. A ten-pound book full of arguments against the justice or reason of this debt would not serve to release him from one penny of obligation. But the child can run and play heedlessly; and if he dies the debt is canceled. Likewise, the child is a potential citizen, but he can grow up, go to college and—in the case of a child prodigy—receive a Ph.D. degree, and yet not be able to vote. But when he comes of age, he must accept his part of the national debt; and he may or may not accept his privileges of citizenship.

What the Scriptures Teach

Very few sober scholars would dismiss the unanimous doctrine of the church both Roman and Protestant as trivial; nevertheless, we must rest everything on the Scriptures. This is always our only support. We simply call attention to history to show how the church has interpreted the texts. For the doctrine of original sin we refer to the discussion elsewhere. Here we are discussing the remains of carnality in the regenerate. The Apostle Paul points out in Romans 7 the struggles of an awakened sinner trying to justify himself by the Law. Though this is not the experience of a regenerated man, it is hardly the normal experience of a man of the world. In another place the Apostle tells us that a regenerate man can have a similar, if not so violent, struggle within. It is of regenerated persons that he writes: "The flesh lusteth against the Spirit, and the Spirit against the flesh: and these are contrary, the one to the other: so that ye cannot do the things that ye would. But if ye be led of the Spirit, ye are not under the law" (Gal. 5:17-18).

According to the doctrine of depravity through deprivation we would interpret the doctrine of depravity in believers as a lack of something. That lack is of the complete image of God, or entire sanctification. The regenerate is a babe in Christ. As such he has much for which to praise. What does he lack? He lacks manhood, obviously. Now he can be a perfect babe without manhood, but he cannot be a perfect man without it, and that is the purpose of God for us according to Scripture. This lack is well noted by the Apostle. Notice that for him this lack is carnality. "And I, brethren, could not speak unto you as unto spiritual, but as unto carnal, even as unto babes in Christ. . . . For ye are yet carnal: for whereas there is among you envying, and strife, and divisions, are ye not carnal, and walk as men?" W. H. Howard, in the *Abingdon Commentary* on this text, says that the Greek term here translated carnal "is more distinctly ethical, 'having the characteristics of flesh,' 'carnally minded.'" And G. B. Stevens says, "It is a moral perversion."*

The writer of the Hebrews addresses regenerate Christians as babes in Christ who have "become such as have need of milk, and not of strong meat" (5:12). Doubtless he is warning against the remains of carnality when he puts them on guard

---

*In *Theology of the New Testament*, p. 345.

"lest any root of bitterness springing up trouble you, and thereby many be defiled" (12:15). Peter regarded the baptism of the Holy Ghost as the means of cleansing out this "root of bitterness." When reporting on the baptism of the Holy Ghost which fell on the house of Cornelius, he compared it to the Spirit baptism of Pentecost which purified the Jewish saints at Jerusalem. God "put no difference between us and them, purifying their hearts by faith" (Acts 15:9). John saw the same glorious possibility for us: "If we walk in the light, as he is in the light, we have fellowship one with another, and the blood of Jesus Christ his Son cleanseth us from all sin" (I John 1:7).

Inadequacy of the Figure

It will be objected that if all the regenerate need is to become men, then growth is all that is necessary. Here the answer is that we are only using a figure of speech, inadequate in more than one respect. It is a scriptural figure, and hence needs no apology, but it is a metaphor, a short parable, meant only to prove the lack in the regenerate but not to prove how that lack is supplied. As a matter of fact there have been babes who were naturally incapable of growing into men. And in the plan of redemption, this must always be the case, because in that plan everything is of grace. Nothing that pertains to redemption can depend upon works or growth. All must be a gift. In Protestant theology it is not simply a paradox, it is a self-contradiction to attribute any feature of redemption to works or growth. It must be a gift of God, or all Protestant theology (and New Testament theology, too) is undermined.

Of course the Scriptures definitely teach growth in grace— but not growth *into* grace. Therefore, growth in grace cannot produce entire sanctification. Moreover, entire sanctification must never be confused with maturity; for by definition, maturity is the end of growth while entire sanctification is the condition most favorable to growth. We grow in grace as long as we live; therefore, we never reach anything more than a relative maturity. It is maturity and not entire sanctification which is reached only at death. Spiritual manhood is only a figurative expression to denote entire sanctification.

Theory of Gradual Sanctification

The theory of gradual sanctification is set forth in the Westminster Confession of Faith, Chapter XIII, as follows:

I. They who are effectually called and regenerated, having a new heart and a new spirit created in them, are further sanctified, really and personally, through the virtue of Christ's death and resurrection, by his Word and Spirit dwelling in them; the dominion of the whole body of sin is destroyed, and the several lusts thereof are more and more weakened and mortified, and they more and more quickened and strengthened, in all saving graces, to the practice of true holiness without which no man shall see the Lord.

II. This sanctification is throughout in the whole man, yet imperfect in this life; there abideth still some remnants of corruption in every part, whence ariseth a continual and irreconcilable war, the flush lusting against the spirit, and the spirit against the flesh.

III. In which war, although the remaining corruption for a time may much prevail, yet, through the continual supply of strength from the sanctifying Spirit of Christ, the regenerate part doth overcome; and so the saints grow in grace, perfecting holiness in the fear of God.

Note that, according to this theory, this process is never finished till at the moment of death the last remains of original sin are suddenly removed, and the perfected saint is admitted to glory. Certain teachings about sanctification do not tell a regenerate Christian how to become sanctified, but attempt to prove that sanctification is impossible during the whole period of probation. And if no sanctification is possible under probation, where else could it logically occur except in some theoretical purgatory? Certainly Protestants would not have a purgatory, but such a doctrine as this demands purgatory for a step of salvation which cannot be made in this life.

Ancient Greek mythology has a character, Sisyphus, who is forever condemned to roll up a hill a great stone which constantly rolls back, making his task incessant. And the gradual theory sets the task of Sisyphus before every regenerate Christian, young or old. If he is a boy twelve years old, he may live in total ignorance of this doctrine, and yet after six months if he dies, he will be wholly sanctified and enter heaven gloriously with almost no effort toward sanctification. If another boy was converted at the same age and lived and worked for sanctification painfully and prayerfully for sixty years, he would not obtain for his sixty years' toil one whit more than his young friend obtained in the hour of death after only six months.

Sanctification is not a thing which a man works for, it is a gift. It is not a thing which a man grows into; it is a gift which he receives. Gradual sanctification is a doctrine of works, but Paul said, "To him that worketh is the reward not reckoned of grace, but of debt" (Rom. 4:4). Not only is the doctrine of gradual sanctification a doctrine of works, it is also a doctrine wherein some work much harder than others for no greater pay. In the illustration given, one man worked sixty years and received not one whit more of sanctification than the youth who scarcely worked at all.

PARABLES OF SANCTIFICATION

No student of psychology should be surprised at the use of parables by our Lord, for the facts and principles of the spiritual life stand entirely alone by themselves. They are unique. It is difficult sometimes to find any resemblance between them and physical phenomena. Take consciousness or mind, for example. We say the lighting up of an electric light is *like it*. Like it, perhaps, but after all how different!

The Reclaimed House

Likewise we may say that entire sanctification is like an owner recovering his house. Here holiness is likened to divine ownership. Through fraud, the house of Man-Soul has been transferred away from its rightful Owner, on the records. The Lawyer (Christ, our Advocate) goes to court and has the house correctly transferred to its rightful Owner (justification). At that moment the rightful Owner takes possession and rebuilds the house (regeneration). Meanwhile some of the old tenant's furniture (carnality) remains. At length the house is rebuilt, the old furniture cast out, and the Owner moves into the building (entire sanctification).

The Reclaimed Slave

In a day when we hate slavery as we do, it is hard to see how it could be a figure of something noble. But if we remember that the finest and highest ideal of human life is that we are God's (divine ownership), perhaps we can adjust our sights to see what the parable means.

The sinner is the fugitive slave of God. Some of our most brilliant theologians maintain that man's root (original) sin is denial of divine sovereignty and the placing of the self in the seat of God. This proposition will stand every theological test. Therefore we say: Man is the fugitive and rebellious slave of God. In the Old Testament we learn of the thing which God owns but cannot use, the *cherem*. At Jericho Joshua was charged to destroy most of the treasure. It belonged to God, and yet God could not use it; it was accursed. Other treasures could come into the treasury. See Joshua 6:17-19. In the Mosaic law the male firstling of every beast belonged to God (Exod. 13:12). Yet since the ass was unclean for sacrifice, the firstling of an ass must be redeemed or killed. And the first born of men must be redeemed (vs. 13).

Man as a fugitive slave from God, is accursed. He cannot consecrate himself, for he already belongs to God (like the unclean ass). He must be redeemed—or perish. The accursed thing in the Mosaic law could not be changed, but the sinner who is alienated and accursed from God, may be changed until he is spiritually a sheep, and as such fit for consecration. "Christ hath redeemed us from the curse of the law . . . for it is written, Cursed is every one that hangeth on a tree" (Gal. 3:13). This explains the text: "For their sakes I sanctify myself that they also may be sanctified through the truth." Christ did not require to be purified from sin, for he "did no sin, neither was guile found in his mouth" (I Pet. 2:22). As our great high priest he was "holy, harmless, undefiled, separate from sinners, and made higher than the heavens" (Heb. 7:26). When he sanctified himself, he consecrated himself to go over on the accursed side of the Book of Judgment, and be made accursed for us. He was not, however, actually alienated from God, for "every devoted [*cherem*, 'accursed'] thing is most holy unto the Lord" (Lev. 27:28).

Creation by Crisis

One indication that the work of redemption cannot be by growth but must be by crisis, is that redemption is a work of creation, and the Book of Genesis shows us the work of creation proceeding, not by natural growth, but by crisis. Ever since the days of Darwin, the scientists have been wrestling with this problem. The word "create" (*bara*, in Hebrew) occurs three times in the creation story, referring (1) to the creation of all matter (1:1); (2) to the creation of animal life (vs. 21); (3) to the creation of man (vs. 27). When it comes to the creation of man, we have two crises: (1) Adam and (2) Eve. This is an answer to the charge that God never does things by halves. As a man Adam was complete, perfect; but as humanity, he lacked something. He was only partially complete—just as the regenerate are incomplete. It is not fantastic to see in the creation of Eve the completion of humanity, and as such a figure of the completion of the work of redemption in humanity.

Various Old Testament Symbols

For many years the journey to Canaan has been highly regarded as a type of the crises of redemption. The Red Sea crossing typifies conversion, and crossing Jordan signifies entire sanctification. Hebrews 4 explains that the Sabbath rest of Genesis is a type of the rest that remaineth for the people of God; namely, full salvation. The same writer sets forth the ancient tabernacle as a type of the experiences of the Christian life. The court represents the convicted state, where penitents find forgiveness at the altar of burnt offering and pass into the holy place, a symbol of conversion. There, the blood having been sprinkled on the horns of the altar of incense, they pass into the holy of holies, type of the sanctified life. See Hebrews 10: 19-21. Christians are exhorted to go on to perfection (6: 1).

The Meaning of Confirmation

Confirmation is the rule in the Roman, Greek, Lutheran, and Episcopal churches. This is a kind of theological fossil, a relic in the modern world of the custom of the apostolic church to lay hands on baptized believers in order that they might receive the baptism of the Holy Spirit which sanctifies the believer (Acts 19: 6; 8: 12-19). For the Spirit's anointing and sealing see I John 2: 27; II Corinthians 1: 21, 22; Ephesians 1: 13; 4: 30. Not that we approve of confirmation, for it is only a lifeless imitation of the ancient custom of consecrating definitely for a second work of grace.

The New Testament had different terms for persons in the two stages of progress in divine grace. In Greek they were *idiotai* (laymen) and *teleios* (perfect). The "laymen" are mentioned as "unlearned" (I Cor. 14: 16, 23-24). Here the Greek term is *idiotai*. In Acts 4: 13 the same term is translated "ignorant" (AV) or "common men" (RSV). The meaning is not ignorant, but nonprofessional, or common. It was the term for a private in the Greek army. The perfect or *teleios* are mentioned in the New Testament in the following passages where the King James Version translates "men" (I Cor. 14: 20); "perfect" (2: 6; Phil. 3: 15; Col. 1: 28; 4: 12); "perfect man" (Eph. 4: 13; Jas. 3: 2); "of full age" (Heb. 5: 14). Paul apparently sometimes held "holiness meetings" with these perfect Christians separate from the whole church. See I Corinthians 2: 6; 14: 23. These "perfect" Christians are identified with the *pneumatika* or "spiritual." Following are the passages wherein *pneumatikos,* always translated "spiritual," is applied to a certain class of Christians in the New Testament: I Cor. 2:15; 3:1; 14:37; Gal. 6:1. The Revised Standard Version has taken note of this distinction between two classes of Christians in the New Testament, but has mistakenly adopted the view that the perfect are distinguished as mature Christians. Maturity is an idea not found in the New Testament but must be injected into it. When a man is mature he stops growing. And New Testament Christians must continue to grow throughout the period of their probation.

"Christian perfection" is a term found often in holiness literature. The Greek word for perfect, *teleios*, differs from the English word perfect. The English word is a superlative, indicating the highest excellence and superiority, whereas the Greek word for perfect simply indicates completion. In the Greek a hut finished is just as perfect as the finest palace ever built. Completion is the idea, and not superlative excellence. The Christian who has been fully possessed by the Holy Spirit has the work of redemption finished. He is therefore perfect in the New Testament sense. He is also holy, inasmuch as he is owned fully by God. If holiness means only divine ownership and possession (and it does), how blasphemous it is for Christians to scoff at it. The Christian who is wholly owned and possessed by God is filled with the love of God. Therefore he is *perfect in love.*

The Baptism of the Holy Ghost

Because of concentrating attention on deliverance from the remains of original sin, the early Wesleyan teachers did not give much thought to the baptism of the Holy Spirit. Our times have seen a great deal of discussion of what happened when the Spirit fell on Pentecost. And even if one has not yet discovered the scriptural doctrine of carnality in believers, there is nevertheless enough in the story of Pentecost to drive him to his knees to pray for a second crisis—the baptism of the Holy Spirit and power. Doubtless tens of thousands have sought and received this baptism. The Keswick Movement in the British Isles has promoted the search for the Spirit baptism in a revival that has spread for generations throughout the British Commonwealth and has enlisted thousands of the clergy and many distinguished bishops and scholars of the Church of England. The point we emphasize is: Get the blessing now; find out what it means later—as soon as you can.

Disciples Converted Before Pentecost

Some, trying to explain Pentecost, have declared that the disciples were not saved before that event. However, in his earthly ministry Jesus had the power to forgive sins: "Son, be of good cheer; thy sins be forgiven thee" (Matt. 9:2). "And he said unto her, Thy sins are forgiven" (Luke 7:47-48). "As many as received him, to them gave he power to become the sons of God" (John 1:12). Christ said they were saved: "Now ye are clean. . . . I am the vine, ye are the branches" (15:3, 5). "Rejoice because your names are written in heaven" (Luke 10:20). Christ had already called them to preach (Matt. 4:18-19; 10:5, 7-8; John 15:16). They preached repentance (Mark 6:12-13).

Christ Promised the Holy Spirit

To these converted men Christ promised: "I will pray the Father, and he shall give you another Comforter, that he may abide with you forever; even the Spirit of truth; whom the world cannot receive" (John 14:16-17). Although the world can receive repentance and salvation, it cannot receive this experience. See John 14:26; 16:7; 15:19; 17:14. Although these disciples were converted men, nevertheless they were not yet perfect in love. They had tormenting fear (Mark 14:50), and "he that feareth is not made perfect in love" (I John 4:18).

Although saved and called to preach, they were not yet sanctified wholly. Therefore Christ prayed: "Sanctify them through thy truth, thy word is truth." The Apostle John often used the word truth as a synonym for reality. Here he means, "Make them holy in reality as they are ceremonially holy."

Some modern Christians are stumbled by the substitution in some of the modern versions of "consecrate" for "sanctify." The Revised Standard Version at first made this change, but when representatives of the Holiness Movement put the arguments before them, they retracted and restored the word "sanctify" in most of the texts. Thereby they acknowledged that we were correct on this point. Even in the Latin Testament "sanctify" is used instead of "consecrate." Consecrate is commonly used in modern church English for what you do for yourself, and "sanctify" indicates what God does for you.

Instances of Holy Spirit Baptism in Acts

First of all comes the great Day of Pentecost when the men who, as we have proved, had been previously converted were baptized by the Holy Spirit and fire (Acts 2:1-12). The believers at Samaria had certainly been converted. They believed on Christ, and were baptized and received great joy (8:5-13). Later, hands were laid on them by the Apostles from Jerusalem, and they "received the Holy Ghost" (8:17). After Paul was converted on the road to Damascus, he entered Damascus and Ananias laid hands on him for the reception of the Holy Spirit (9:17). At Ephesus Paul prayed for some twelve disciples, "and the Holy Ghost came on them" (19:6). Sometimes there was no laying on of hands. At the home of Cornelius "the Holy Ghost fell on all them which heard the word" (10:44). Cornelius was already a believer, a devout man as was doubtless his household.

How Is Entire Sanctification Received?

In our study of justification we found that the sole condition of justification is, and must be, faith alone, but that faith cannot be exercised by the impenitent. Accepting the principle that no gift of grace can be earned, that all must come by faith, we agree that entire sanctification is not of works, but of faith. Nevertheless, it is a faith which follows consecration. Here we shall use "consecration" to indicate the dedication of himself which a Christian makes, and "sanctification" as the work of the Holy Spirit when he takes full possession of the believer with the latter's consent and desire, and fills him with the fullness of love and power.

Sanctifying the Holy

Most people find some difficulty in understanding how it is possible to sanctify (or consecrate) believers who are already admittedly holy. Light is shed on this by remembering that the primary meaning of holiness is belonging to God, but belonging, or ownership, is not completed till full possession is gained. The vilest sinner belongs to God in deepest reality, but the devil claims ownership. As in the parable of the house whose owner is dispossessed, when Christ dispossesses the devil, the title is transferred to God, and the sinner is justified and is ceremonially holy. God has ownership, but it takes another act of the court to give God full possession and oust the devil's last piece of furniture. Then the house not only belongs to God, but is in full possession of God, which means entire sanctification.

There is a sense by which men sanctify (consecrate) a thing which is already holy by their deep heartfelt acknowledgment of its holiness. This idea of consecration, or sanctification, is prominent in the Old Testament. Moses and Aaron were rebuked for not sanctifying God before Israel (Num. 20:12; 27:14). Israel was commanded to sanctify the Sabbath (Deut. 5:12). "The first born . . . it is mine" (Exod. 13:2). The people were commanded to sanctify the house of the Lord God (II Chron. 29:5). Instances of this kind are found elsewhere in the Old Testament. And in the New Testament we are commanded to pray. "Hallowed be thy name," which means to sanctify the name of God. The Wesleyan theologians taught that sanctification begins in regeneration. The second crisis experience is the reception of entire sanctification. While all Christians are holy in a ceremonial sense, they are not all wholly so in a moral sense, in the experience of moral purity.

What Is Christian Consecration?

We have seen that penitent sinners on first coming to God
are called to repentance and faith. The Christian believer un-
dertakes the work of entire consecration because he would
confirm by the deep consent of his own will that ownership of
God which is already implicit in his acceptance as a Christian.
Such acceptances are common to life. One moves to a faraway
land and lives there, sometimes for years, before accepting his
fate; so people adjust to the Army, to a new job, to marriage.

"I beseech you therefore, brethren, by the mercies of God,
that ye present your bodies a living sacrifice, holy, acceptable
unto God, which is your reasonable service" (Rom. 12:1).
Some have tried to make this text teach a repetitious dedication of oneself in the oft-repeated worship of the Christian congregation. But here the tense is in the aorist, which indicates a
once-for-all transaction—a thing not repeated. This act of consecration is the dedication of a priest to continuous service in
the temple of God; for we are all made priests: "And hath
made us kings and priests unto God" (Rev. 1:6). "Ye . . . are
. . . an holy priesthood" (I Pet. 2:5); "a royal priesthood" (vs.
9). This service is not one oft repeated; it is a perpetual ministry. "They . . . serve him day and night in his temple" (Rev.
7:15). Paul expresses it, "Instantly serving God day and
night" (Acts 26:7).

Again we are exhorted to "yield yourselves unto God, as
those that are alive from the dead, and your members as instruments of righteousness unto God" (Rom. 6:13). Here the
verb "yield" is the same as the one translated "present" in
12:1. It means to dedicate or consecrate. The verb here is also
in the aorist tense, meaning a thing done once for all—like the
act of death itself. However, the second word of 6:13 is the
same verb used in the present tense: "Neither yield . . . unto
sin." Here it means continuous surrender to sin. The whole
verse might be rendered: "Neither repeatedly yield ye your
members as instruments of unrighteousness unto sin; but once

for all consecrate yourselves unto God as those that are alive from the dead." The devil is pleased with repeated yielding; God demands "once-for-all consecration"—not frequent reconsecration. We find the same idea elsewhere. "To offer up spiritual sacrifices" (I Pet. 2:5) is in the aorist tense, signifying offerings made once for all.

Indeed, there are sacrifices which the Christian offers up repeatedly: "Let us offer the sacrifice of praise to God continually" (Heb. 13:15). Here the verb is in the present tense. The famous New Testament commentator, Dean Henry Alford, says on I Peter 2:5: ". . . **to offer up** (no habitual offering, as in rite or festival, is meant, but the one, once-for-all devotion of the body, as in Rom. xii. 1, to God as His)." Another consecration text is this: "Having therefore these promises, dearly beloved, let us cleanse ourselves from all filthiness of the flesh and spirit, perfecting holiness in the fear of God" (II Cor. 7:1). This is a renunciation of the remains of carnality. It is the same as "the superfluity of naughtiness" which a truly great scholar like Theodore Zahn in his *Introduction to the New Testament* does not hesitate to translate "residue-remainder," following Mark 8:8. He adds: "The writer means the old, hereditary faults which still cling even to those born of God."

Old Testament Word for "Consecrate"

Five Hebrew terms are translated "consecrate" in the King James Old Testament: (1) to devote (used once); (2) to separate (three times); (3) to set apart (seven times); (4) to fill the hand (eighteen times); (5) filling up (eleven times). This is approximate, as many forms of these words are used. We note that the most widely used of these terms is the one which means "to fill the hand." This is a reference to the custom of filling the hands of the new priest with the sacrificial offering for his priestly service. This is the act which confers authority to function upon him. The first offering in the hands of the regenerate Christian is his own body to be sacrificed "once for all." The love of God, "agape" in the Greek New Testament, is a devotion which pursues us, not for what we can give, but for what he can do for us. His holiness seeks us to possess us, and his love seeks us to fill and bless us. These both overtake us in the blessing of perfect love.

Consecration: Gradual or Complete?

Just at the moment when it seemed possible to escape from the traditional doctrine of gradual sanctification we ran into a popular doctrine of gradual consecration. This is characterized by the traditional repetitiousness of medieval Christianity which denied certitude and emphasized repeated confessions of sins and continuous professions of consecration. This religion is afflicted with relativity. But in secular things the mind of man is concerned with absolutes. He is either alive or dead. He is guilty or innocent. He is married or unmarried. He is a citizen or an alien. Likewise he is capable of complete consecration, even when he is ignorant of the future and of its demands.

Often we are told that one must make a new consecration every time he meets with a new demand on his Christian consecration. This is false. Is not a man as fully married at the moment he walks away from the altar as on the day of his golden wedding anniversary? He is. He never needs to marry the same person again. Sometimes we hear the doctrine of gradual sanctification preached among us as the theory of unconsecrated areas in our lives which must be consecrated as we come to them. In marriage this theory would call for a new wedding every six months or oftener.

Faith Is the Condition

We believe that faith is the key to every door of grace, to every advance in the work of redemption. It is an axiom of evangelical theology that all the redemptive work of Christ is a gift, and as such it is not attainable as a reward of merit, or as pay for vast labor or painful work, but is a gracious favor given into the hands of active and childlike faith. The only work which God requires for the reception of his redemption blessing is faith. "This is the work of God, that ye believe on him whom he hath sent" (John 6:29). Paul was a wholly sanctified man, and this is his method: "I am crucified with Christ: nevertheless I live; yet not I, but Christ liveth in me: and the life which I now live in the flesh I live by the faith of the Son of God" (Gal. 2:20). "And put no difference between us and them, purifying their hearts by faith" (Acts 15:9). Here faith was the means whereby they found the blessing. "That they may receive forgiveness of sins, and inheritance among them which are sanctified by faith that is in me" (26:18). See also I John 3:3 and II Thessalonians 2:13.

Chapter VII

CHRIST AS HEALER

HEALING IN THE GOSPEL

The traditional theory of Protestantism concerning healing is that Christ performed miracles to prove his spiritual message; and after the apostolic age miracles ceased forever. This theory is tending to dissolve away in our time, inasmuch as even liberals tend to believe that wonders of mind healing may occur in the church of our time. Christ exercised a ministry of healing. "Jesus went about all Galilee, teaching in their synagogues, and preaching the gospel of the kingdom, and healing all manner of sickness and all manner of disease among the people. And his fame went throughout all Syria: and they brought unto him all sick people that were taken with divers diseases and torments, and those which were possessed with devils, and those which were lunatic, and those that had the palsy; and he healed them."

This healing was set in the church as a perpetual ordinance: "Is any sick among you? let him call for the elders of the church; and let them pray over him, anointing him with oil in the name of the Lord: and the prayer of faith shall save the sick, and the Lord shall raise him up; and if he have committed sins, they shall be forgiven him" (Jas. 5:14-16). Physical health may well be consistent with soul health: "I wish above all things that thou mayest prosper and be in health, even as thy soul prospereth" (III John 2).

Nearly all heathen religion, ancient and modern, was concerned with bodily health. Savage medicine men pretend to heal their tribesmen. And the educated heathen of Greece and Rome went to the priests in the temples for healing. The ministry of healing has never ceased in the Church of Rome and is spreading widely throughout modern Protestantism, especially among some of the smaller sects. At the same time most of the cults promote mind healing.

MIRACLE AND NATURAL LAW

In all the present-day talk about faith healing, mind healing, psychiatry, and so forth, it is important to make clear distinctions. Medical healing is by the use of drugs, physical appliances and methods. Psychiatric healing is healing through the mind, as the word indicates. Divine healing is healing by a miracle of God in response to the prayer of faith. It is always a miracle.

As we have explained elsewhere, a miracle is an act of God which takes place in the divine self-consciousness. Here we do not mean that God is ever unconscious of his acts (far from it), but in order to explain the difference between God's immanence (or the way we behold God functioning in nature) and the divine transcendence (the way we see God working in grace), we adopt a figure of speech comparing the immanence of God to human subconscious behavior, or the automatic functioning of the sympathetic nervous system, and the transcendence of God we liken to the self-consciousness of the human mind. In this way we see the immanent God working in nature by what we suppose are the uniform laws of nature (I say "suppose"—for who knows that much about the universe?). Now medical healing is on the level of nature; such also is psychiatric healing, in reality. Divine healing is a miracle of faith.

A miracle is whatever God intends to do in his creative freedom, not simply in accordance with the uniformity of natural law. This does not require the violation of natural law, but the intentional use of it. I flew across the Atlantic three times, and while these were not miraculous journeys, they were certainly not events which would have happened without manipulating natural law. We believe God can likewise manipulate uniform natural law to bring about intended effects in the realm of the supernatural, the transcendent, or the self-consciousness of God.

DIVINE HEALING IN THE ATONEMENT

There has been considerable debate in our midst over whether divine healing is in the atonement. For us the answer is settled in the Book of God. "With his stripes we are healed" (Isa. 53:5). During his earthly ministry Christ "healed all that were sick: that it might be fulfilled which was spoken by Esaias the prophet, saying, Himself took our infirmities, and bare our sicknesses" (Matt. 8:16-17).

Certain teachers have drawn such enormous conclusions from this doctrine that many have denied the doctrine, instead of waiting to understand it. For example, we have been told: Healing for the body and healing for the soul are on exactly the same basis. If you do not receive healing, it is because you do not have enough faith; and if you lack faith, it is because your obedience is defective. You have some stain of sin on your soul. You know that you do not have faith enough for bodily healing; how can you think you do have enough faith to heal your soul? Through many years I have seen this line of reasoning torture good Christians more terribly than would the strokes of a steel lash. What is illogical about this theory?

Death and Disease Came by Sin

Elsewhere we have brought out the truth that Adam was offered a divine defense against death in the Garden of Eden. He was thrust out of Eden, "lest he put forth his hand, and take also of the tree of life, and eat, and live forever" (Gen. 3:22). That is to say, although death had existed among the animals for ages, man was the fair child of God, and was created with the gift of life just within his grasp, so long as he lived in obedience and by faith. Paul teaches this as plainly as words can do so. In Romans 5 the theme is worked out

fully: Death came by sin. "Wherefore, as by one man sin
entered into the world, and death by sin; and so death passed
upon all men, for that all have sinned" (vs. 12). This text alone
should be enough to prove that healing and the redemption of
the body are within the atonement; otherwise there would be
no resurrection from the dead. Death, then, says Paul, is
caused by sin, and if death, then all sickness and disease, for
disease and death are but two sides of the same coin. No disease, no death; no death, no disease. Disease (any kind) is
the beginning of death. And death is always the completion of
disease. When an automobile wrecks, the injured occupants
are abruptly thrown into an abnormal physical condition exactly equivalent to disease.

It would not be illogical to suppose that this sentence of
death was canceled immediately at the moment of conversion,
and Paul found heretics who did so teach in his day, "saying
that the resurrection is past already" (II Tim. 2:18). But Paul
denounced them as having erred from the truth. The writer
of Hebrews taught the true doctrine: "It is appointed unto
men once to die, but after this the judgment" (9:27). It is the
universal faith of Christendom that this final cancellation of
all the penalties and consequences of sin is at the resurrection;
and so Paul teaches: "Not only they, but ourselves also, which
have the first fruits of the Spirit, even we ourselves groan
within ourselves, waiting for the adoption, to wit, the redemption of our body" (Rom. 8:23).

There is not space to develop the thought fully, but the truth
is that we partake of the full benefits of the redemption of
the soul from sin here and now, in this life; but the redemption
of our body completely from disease and death is postponed till
the resurrection. Divine healing is a kind of first fruits of the
experience of glorification when death shall be finally overcome, and we shall be made partakers of the resurrected life
of Christ.

God's Will Determinative

God sometimes sends affliction and disease. Many deny that God ever sends sickness or disease. We have no argument with such. Their debate is with the Bible which repeats again and again the fact that it is so. "Who maketh the dumb, or deaf, or the seeing, or the blind? have not I the Lord?" (Exod. 4:11). "I will even appoint over you terror, consumption, and the burning ague" (Lev. 26:16). "Then the Lord will make thy plagues wonderful . . . even great plagues . . . and sore sicknesses. . . . Moreover he will bring upon thee all the diseases of Egypt, which thou wast afraid of. . . . Every sickness, and every plague, which is not written in the book of this law, them will the Lord bring upon thee" (Deut. 28:59-61). "Therefore will I make thee sick in smiting thee" (Mic. 6:13).

God sometimes withholds healing. "But I tell you of a truth, many widows were in Israel in the days of Elias, . . . but unto none of them was Elias sent, save unto Sarepta. . . . And many lepers were in Israel in the time of Eliseus the prophet; and none of them was cleansed, saving Naaman the Syrian" (Luke 4:25-27). These are the words of Christ, teaching that there is a selectivity in the work of healing and miracle far beyond our feeble logic. Elisha passed hundreds of godly Israelitish widows dying with the white fire of famine on their lips to take miracle bread to a heathen widow. And hundreds of pious Israelites rotted with the foul ulcers of leprosy while Elias' visitor—a heathen general—passed them on his way to healing at the prophet's hands. Even Jesus must often have passed the lame man at the temple gate, who later was healed by Peter and John; and Paul, a miracle worker, left Trophimus at Miletum sick (II Tim. 4:20).

Healing is of faith, but it must be according to the will of God. The writer was brought up on the theory that the successful prayer of faith always means getting what you want out of life, but when Christ prayed for what he could not have, he added, "Nevertheless, not my will, but thine be done."

Chapter VIII

CHRIST, THE HEAD OF THE CHURCH

MEANING OF THE WORD "CHURCH"

With only one exception (Acts 19:37, where "robbers of churches" means "temple robbers") the English word "church" in the King James Version of the New Testament is translated from the Greek word *ekklesia,* which simply means "called out," or "the called out ones." This was an expression long in use in Greek literature to denote the political assembly of the Greek city-state. Later it came to be applied to meetings quite generally. It has so much more meaning in the New Testament use that its simple etymological definition is quite inadequate.

Several centuries before the beginning of the Christian Era the Jewish people began to be dispersed throughout most of the countries around the Mediterranean, northward throughout Roman-occupied Europe, and eastward to the edges of China. Nearly everywhere the Jews learned to speak Greek, and soon the Old Testament was translated from Hebrew into the Greek language. This Greek Old Testament, called the Septuagint, was spread everywhere among the Jewish synagogues of the Dispersion, and finally of Palestine itself. Its use was common among the early Christians. The Hebrew Old Testament had several words for "congregation." The two most common were *edah* and *quahal.* In the Greek version of the Old Testament *edah* was translated *synagogos* and *quahal* (found eighty-one times) was translated *ekklesia.* Says Professor C. C. Richardson:

It is the Hebrew background of the word, however, that was determinative for the Early Church. In later Judaism there were two terms used

119

of the people of Israel. One signified the local congregation of Jews in any given place (synagogue); the other meant the ideal Israel, the whole body of those who had been called by God to salvation. It was this latter Hebrew term which was translated by the Greek *ekklesia,* and in this particular sense it was used by the Christians. They regarded themselves as the true Israel, the remnant which was faithful and had been called of God.[1]

It is important to note that the early Christians took this name right out of their Old Testament to show the whole religious world of their time that they professed to be the new and true Israel of God, the true remnant of Israel spoken of in the Prophets. In my *The Apostolic Church* (pp. 99-104) I have given convincing evidence of this fact. Premillennialists say one cannot understand the Bible until he can distinguish the church from Israel. The fact is, no one can understand the Bible until he learns that the church is identical with spiritual Israel.

The great Swiss theologian Emil Brunner has recently written:

The ecclesia of Jesus Christ is God's people, the elect people—that was also the rightful description of Israel. . . . And yet the fellowship founded by Jesus realized that it was something wholly new, namely the fellowship of those who through Jesus Christ share in the New Covenant, and the new aeon.[2]

In a new book describing the developments of modern theology, Professor Daniel Day Williams writes:

The church is the company of those who have the new life because this [conversion] has happened to them. . . . To be in Christ is to be in the church. They are interdependent. Of course Church here does not mean simply an institution and its formal boundaries of membership. It means the corporate body of believers. God's word in Christ saves us just by bringing us within such a body where life is shared, sustained and renewed in a loving relationship to others. Christ is the one head of this new people which is in its essence catholic, that is "universal and whole."[3]

---

[1]From *The Church Through the Centuries* by C. C. Richardson, p. 19. Used by permission of Charles Scribner's Sons.
[2]From *The Misunderstanding of the Church* by Emil Brunner, pp. 19-20. Copyright, 1953, by W. L. Jenkins, The Westminster Press. Used by permission.
[3]From *What Present Day Theologians Are Thinking* by Daniel Day Williams, pp. 18, 129. Used by permission of Harper & Brothers.

DENOMINATIONALISM NOT THE CHURCH

It stands to reason that if the church is the whole body of Christ, then no denomination dare lay claim to be the church or even a church. This fact is coming to be acknowledged almost universally today. Dr. C. C. Morrison, long-time editor of the *Christian Century*, says:

> Of the one church which God gave us, man has made many churches. These churches all embody human self-will and each exists in contravention of the will of Christ. The true church is free because its allegiance is given to Christ who is its head. But the denomination is not free, because, in its apostasy from the true church, it is not under Christ. This is instinctively recognized by our evangelical denominations not one of which would claim that Christ is the head of its denomination. . . . Here again we confront the sin of which the ecumenical movement penitently confesses that we stand in need of divine forgiveness. It is the sin of absolutizing the independence and autonomy of a fragment of the church over against the true Church of Christ.[4]

On this point Professor Williams writes:

> The true church is not only greater than any one of the organized churches, but is greater than all of them.[5]

Persons familiar with modern theological literature will know that these quotations are only fragments of a vast mass which could be quoted to prove both that denominationalism is not the church and that it is sinful, since it divides the true church which is the holy body of Christ. "And hath put all things under his feet, and gave him to be the head over all things to the church, which is his body, the fullness of him that filleth all in all" (Eph. 1:22-23). "Christ is the head of the church: and he is the savior of the body" (5:23). "And he is the head of the body, the church" (Col. 1:18). "Not holding the Head, from which all the body by joints and bands having nourishment ministered, and knit together, increaseth with the increase of God" (Col. 2:19).

[4]From *The Unfinished Reformation* by Charles Clayton Morrison, pp. 78-79. Used by permission of Harper & Brothers.
[5]Williams, *op. cit.*, p. 145.

VISIBLE AND INVISIBLE CHURCH

Adolf Harnack, the famous German church historian, says that the apostolic church and the generations following never acknowledged any distinction between the visible and the invisible church. Augustine is credited with originating that idea. He was sharply criticized by a widespread denomination of his time, called the Donatists. They said the Catholics could not be the church of God, for the true church is holy, whereas there were many ungodly persons in the fellowship of the Catholic Church, even back in the fourth century. It was then that Augustine invented the famous distinction between the visible and invisible church. There were, he admitted, members in the visible catholic church who were not actually members of the invisible church of Christ.

This distinction was allowed to slumber for a thousand years. When finally, the Roman Catholic theologians condemned the Protestants in the sixteenth century for splitting and dividing the church, the latter did not retort, as they might have done, that the Roman and Greek churches had actually begun the process of division back in the ninth century, completing it in the eleventh century by leaving the pope's anathema upon the altar of the Greek Cathedral of Saint Sophia in Constantinople. Instead the Protestant theologians fell back upon the famous defense of Augustine, and asserted that they had not actually divided the body of Christ, but had only split the visible church. Protestant theology emphasized this distinction between the visible and invisible church for many generations. At last there are signs of a change of mind in modern Protestant theology. Emil Brunner says: "The idea of the invisible church is foreign to the New Testament."[6]

William Adams Brown, famous theologian of the recent past, wrote:

A distinction is frequently made in theology between the church visible, and the church invisible; the former term being used to denote the

---

[6]Brunner, *op. cit.*, p. 9.

ecclesiastical organization, the latter the company of the elect who shall finally be saved. . . . But it must never be suffered to obscure the fact that the church of Christ exists today as a definite body in the persons of the men and women who have been touched by his Spirit, and who live for the ends which he approves. This spiritual society, creating institutions, but not itself perfectly comprehended or expressed by any, is the true church of Christ.[7]

The New Testament knows no such distinction as a visible and invisible church, for there the church is only one body. We might liken it to the figure of a man. An invisible man is not a man; he is a ghost. A visible man without the invisible man is not a man; he is a corpse. The things which the world counts necessary to visibility are likely to be carnal things which impair the church's existence. However, the things which tend to increase the visibility of the church are its good works of worship, witness, and charity. "Let your light so shine before men, that they may see your good works, and glorify your Father which is in heaven" (Matt. 5:16). This is the way to make the church visible. When we see a human body at work and in motion, we know the invisible element is present. Just so the reality of the invisible church is made manifest by its works of love.

THE CHURCH, ONE BODY IN CHRIST

Most alert Christians know today that all forward-looking Christian thinkers in the world are becoming aroused to the danger of division in the church. The sin of division has been denounced in the Bible all along; it is only recently that Protestants have become awakened to the reality of these denunciations.

Oneness in Christ is the universal teaching of the New Testament. "There is neither Jew nor Greek, there is neither bond nor free, there is neither male nor female: for ye are all one in Christ Jesus" (Gal. 3:28). "For both he that sanctifieth and they who are sanctified are all of one" (Heb. 2:11). "For as we have many members in one body . . . so we, being many,

---

[7]From *Christian Theology in Outline* by William Adams Brown, pp. 58-59. Used by permission of Charles Scribner's Sons.

are one body in Christ, and every one members one of another" (Rom. 12: 4-5). "Stand fast in one spirit, with one mind striving together for the faith of the gospel" (Phil. 1: 27). "Now I beseech you, brethren, by the name of our Lord Jesus Christ, that ye all speak the same thing, and that there be no divisions among you; but that ye be perfectly joined together in the same mind and in the same judgment" (I Cor. 1: 10). "Now I beseech you, brethren, mark them which cause divisions and offenses contrary to the doctrine which ye have learned; and avoid them" (Rom. 16: 17).

And now comes the heart-searching prayer of our Lord in the Garden of Gethsemane, on the night of his betrayal. "Neither pray I for these alone, but for them also that shall believe on me through their word; that they all may be one; as thou, Father, art in me, and I in thee, that they also may be one in us: that the world may believe that thou hast sent me" (John 17: 20-21). The world can only believe what it sees; therefore this unity which will make the world believe must be a visible unity.

When we remember how easy it is for trained and active minds to twist and distort texts, I think it is a tribute to the generality of modern theologians that they do not try to evade the awful force of these texts against division. It is the urge of these texts upon the conscience which is furnishing much of the motive force for the present-day movements toward unity. In fact, most denominational mergers have been motivated in this way. This is so much improvement over the old days when these texts were explained as having relevance only to the truly spiritual invisible church.

MEMBERSHIP IN THE CHURCH

Baptism Is Not the Door

Most of the older churches receive members by baptism. In the Apostolic church, regeneration was correctly regarded as the door into the church. After a few generations magical ideas crept in with the multitudes of ignorant people who poured into the Christian fellowship.

Magic pervaded the entire ceremonial life of the church of the third and fourth centuries. The water of baptism literally washed away sin. The believer was regenerated by its cleansing touch and thereby inducted into the church. Likewise, the bread and wine were believed to be changed into the body and blood of Christ. This magic continues in the Church of Rome till the present time. By it the priest, even though a sinner, can forgive the sins of his fellow sinners. He can bless candles and holy water and make the house of worship a holy place (he thinks). Now it is perfectly logical for a believer in magical baptismal regeneration to believe that baptism is the door into the church. Likewise, it is just as illogical for those who believe that regeneration is by faith to accept the idea that water baptism can be the door into the church.

We Enter by Regeneration

The ancient Anabaptists taught that regeneration makes one a member of the kingdom of God, whereas the church is a special group of believers who constitute themselves a church by entering a pledged fellowship. No one is a member of this church except those who have entered its covenant of fellowship. Some churches continue to believe a theory like this and elect new members to their fellowship by a democratic vote. This view completely surrenders the idea that the church is the body of Christ and that membership therein is equivalent to salvation.

It is a common doctrine of Protestantism that salvation makes a person a member of the universal, invisible, spiritual church but is quite insufficient to make one a member of the local congregation. Logically this is to deny that the local church is also a part of the universal church. But if not, why not? And to what church does it belong?

Local Church Membership the Key

Let us become realistic here. Many persons will object to close thinking at this point, claiming that it is an unimportant piece of theorizing. But at this point we must find the solution of the church's age-old division or else admit that its unity is forever impossible. It may be regarded as proved by the experience of the ages that unless we can come by a new understanding of local church membership, universal church unity is impossible forever. No number of denominations can by human organization create the mystical body of Christ, the church. No denomination is that church, and all of them together can never constitute that spiritual fellowship.

The church of the Apostolic age was never a human organization or legal corporation. It was always and only a spiritual fellowship composed of believers in Christ. Unless we can recover this insight, unity is forever impossible. The New Testament teaches that a man who is a member of the body of Christ is at the same time essentially and of right a member of every one of its local congregations without joining. If because of false accusations, a given congregation should refuse to acknowledge his membership, that would be an abnormality and would temporarily limit his privileges in that congregation, but it would not essentially alter the great spiritual facts.

The experience of Paul himself furnishes an example: "And when Saul was come to Jerusalem, he assayed to join himself to the disciples: but they were all afraid of him, and believed not that he was a disciple. But Barnabas took him, and brought him to the apostles, and declared unto them how he had seen the Lord in the way, and that he had spoken to him, and how he had preached boldly at Damascus in the name of Jesus. And he was with them coming in and going out at Jerusalem" (Acts 9:26-28). The contention is made that Paul tried to join the Jerusalem church and failed until endorsed by Barnabas. The facts are quite otherwise. The Greek word translated "join" here is elsewhere rendered "to keep company" (10:28);

"cleave unto" (17:34); "cleaveth" (Luke 10:11). Even where it is translated "join" the context does not indicate the act of joining an organization, but means rather "to associate with": as the Prodigal Son "joined himself to a citizen" (15:15). "Go near, and join thyself to this chariot" (Acts 8:29).

Weymouth translates Acts 9:26: "He . . . made several attempts to associate with the disciples." In other words, Paul knew that as a Christian he already belonged to the Jerusalem local church; therefore he attempted to associate with them. But they, knowing that he had been a former spy of the Sanhedrin and had dragged men and women off to prison and death, were naturally afraid of him. He showed no resentment at this natural fear and went to find a trusted brother—not to prove that he was worthy to join, but that he already belonged to the Jerusalem church, even though all its gifted leaders mistrusted him. Even the rejection of eleven apostles and scores of elders could not throw him out of a church which was his by faith and divine grace alone. It is illogical to think that any member of the church of God would have anything to do to join any local congregation anywhere.

Universal Membership

Sir William Ramsay, authority on the apostolic church, in describing Paul's conception of the church writes:

That was a conception analogous to the Roman view, that every group of Roman citizens meeting together in a body . . . in any part of the vast Empire formed a part of the great conception "Rome," and that such a group was not an intelligible idea, except as a piece of the great unity. Any Roman citizen who came to any provincial town where such a group existed was forthwith a member of the group; and the group was simply a fragment of "Rome," cut off in space from the whole body, but preserving its vitality and self-identity as fully as when it was joined to the whole, and capable of reuniting with the whole as soon as the estranging space was annihilated. Such was the Roman constitutional theory, and such was the Pauline theory. . . . The Pauline theory was carried out with a logical . . . consistency which the Roman theory could never attain in practice.[8]

---

[8]In *St. Paul the Traveler and the Roman Citizen* (Putnam), pp. 125-6.

Let us remember that this is also the doctrine of citizenship framed into the fundamental law of the United States of America. The Constitution provides: "The citizens of each State shall be entitled to all privileges and immunities of citizens in the several States" (Art. IV: sec. 2, clause 1). After the Civil War the following amendment was added: "All persons born or naturalized in the United States, and subject to the jurisdiction thereof, are citizens of the United States and of the State wherein they reside" (Art. XIV; sec. 1). In other words a citizen of the United States at large is free to reside in any state he may choose, and is by inalienable right a citizen of any such state. A citizen of Chicago, for instance, may go wherever he pleases and reside in and claim the right to vote in any voting precinct of the United States without joining anything anywhere. This is the spiritual privilege of a child of God in the church. Adolf Harnack, J. Weiss, F. C. Grant, as well as many others have expressed views similar to those of Ramsay quoted above.

Figures Used by Christ

Christ says: "I am the vine, ye are the branches" (John 15:5). Some have tried to make the branches signify denominations, but such homemade exegesis cannot withstand the light of modern knowledge. Christ says: "If a man abide not in me, he is cast forth as a branch, and is withered." Each branch is a human individual. This parable sets forth the intimate relation of the church members to the Head of the church. Only sin can excommunicate them. They base their church membership frankly in him alone. They draw their churchly life from him, in fellowship with the other branches.

Again Christ says: "I am the good shepherd." He also claims to be the door, and to have one fold (John 10:7, 16). Here the church is both a flock and a fold. All the sheep are objects of a love that is ready to give its life in their defense. The exalted moral idealism of the parables of our Lord have touched the hearts of the finest of men. He spoke to the lowly and the humble. Upon his parables is the dew of wheat fields and meadow, the odor of harvest, the beauty of common things. He took the ordinary scenes of barnyard and field and home, and when he held them up to the warm sun of truth one saw the moving splendor of Jerusalem the Golden.

Take the intimate little parable of the hen and her brood (Matt. 23:37). Not one orator in a thousand could have lifted that parable to the lofty dignity it holds in the majestic peroration in Christ's lament over the lost Holy City. Shining forever in splendor as a figure of his love for the lost and doomed capital, its plainest and simplest lesson has been generally missed. Just as Christ likens his followers to sheep elsewhere, here he, with no loss of dignity, likens them to little chickens. This figure would seem absurd to any lacking the humility which Christ presupposes for its understanding. The fellowship of the chickens is free; it is based on their nature. It is open to all. The sheep have to go through a door, signifying the narrowness of the way of life. The chickens can find warmth and fellowship as they approach from any direction, signifying the universal appeal of the true spiritual church for her children everywhere.

Gulfs in the Eternal Sea

We must always bear in mind that each local church is like a small pool after a shower. Although it is only tiny, it reflects the glory of sun and sky. Just so each small congregation is a full replica of the universal church. In it is the eternal trinity, the hosts of angels, and the entire spiritual fellowship of all the saints in light. Every redeemed soul in heaven and earth belongs to each small congregation. And the throne of the Highest is there. It is a church of God, because each Person in the Holy Trinity is concerned with it. It is the church of the Holy Ghost, because the Holy Spirit has called out all its members and regenerated them. It is the church of the Father, because "God so loved the world that he gave. . . ." It is the church of Christ, for Christ also loved the church, and the church is his body. Therefore we must call it the church of God, as it is twelve times called in the New Testament. That name witnesses to the work of the triune God in its establishment and ownership.

If the universal church is the eternal sea of the redeemed of all ages, then each true church of God is a gulf in that eternal sea. Now if you build a dam across the mouth of a gulf so as to shut out the fish and the tides, then your gulf is no longer a part of the sea. It is a pond—your pond—no matter how vast it may be. And so it is the stern duty of every local congregation to keep itself open to every true Christian in the world. It must not raise a creed or set a condition of membership which denies that any child of God is essentially a member whenever he chooses to exercise his right. It is that simple— and that difficult. This means that the church, as the church, cannot be organized.

Organizing the Work of the Church

Although the church is the body of Christ, and as such cannot be organized, this does not forbid us to organize the work of the church. Christ organized two committees to carry on his work: the Seventy (Luke 10:1) and the Twelve (Matt. 10:2). We notice that while there is not one unsaved person in the church of God which is the body of Christ, yet in a human organization like the Twelve, there was one who was a traitor —and this may happen in any committee organized even by good men. The apostles organized a committee to administer the charity of the Jerusalem church (Acts 6:1-6). Paul was once sent on a committee to Jerusalem for instruction from the leaders of the church (15:2). Again committees were organized to gather funds from the Gentile churches to care for the poor saints at Jerusalem (I Cor. 16:3; II Cor. 8:19, 23). These examples are sufficient warrant for organizing the Sunday schools and business phases of the local church and standing committees and boards for the connectional work of the church in home and foreign missions, education, publication, and the like.

The Government of the Church

The Church of Rome and the Eastern Orthodox Churches hold that the council of the apostles ruled the church during their lifetime and committed to the bishops their authority over the church throughout all time to come. This authority was transmitted to the successors of the apostles by the touch of the hands of apostles and bishops down to our own time, and to world's end. This doctrine is widely held in the Church of England, in the Protestant Episcopal Church in the United States, and in other old churches. It is a doctrine of magic, entirely without support, except for superstition. Yet it is so sternly held that its advocates cannot dream of a united ecumenical church, unless such a church be ruled by the bishops of the Apostolic Succession.

God Endowed for Leadership

Among the other denominations a widely held theory declares that all kinds of ecclesiastical government are to be found in the apostolic church, such as a church without officials, a church ruled by elders alone, and a church ruled by a monarchial bishop. This theory is too elaborate for such a simple situation as faced the apostolic church. That church had, as Neander long ago asserted, a charismatic government, from the Greek *charisma*, a gift—here understood to be divine. To sum up, the church was *led*—not *ruled*—by persons believed to be called to, and endowed for, their leadership by the Holy Spirit. Their authority lay simply in their ability to influence others, and they were elevated to their positions and retained them by some simple manifestation of democratic control—sometimes by balloting, and again, apparently by general consent. Lifetime tenure in office came much later than the apostolic age.

The variety of form in the constitution of the congregations of the apostolic period was entirely due to the fact that, so to speak, the camera of the writer of Acts caught them at various stages of democratic development. New churches had not yet chosen any officials. Later they chose a body of elders. A body of elders will not conduct the public worship of the church long before one elder begins to take the leadership.

The Rise of the Pastor

Students should not be too much impressed by this single pastor's lofty (in modern terms) title of bishop, say of Antioch or of Ephesus. That means in the language of that time that he was simply the single (monarchial) pastor (bishop) of the local congregation.

For generations most of these pastors lived in deep poverty. Some were fish peddlers; others survived by the humblest means. The bishop (pastor) of a city of 100,000 Christians would always be an impressive figure. But in the early ages, the Christians had no church houses—not till the end of the third century. They worshiped in halls and schoolrooms and in the private homes of their members. For ages the bishop was simply the pastor of one congregation. Eventually one man became bishop of a diocese. Then came archbishops, patriarchs, and then the pope of Rome, and the patriarch of Constantinople—heads respectively of the Western (Latin) and Eastern Orthodox (Greek) churches.

In I Corinthians 12:28 the Apostle lists a number of gifts of the Spirit. Several of these have stimulated large discussion and controversy—tongues, for example. Up till the rise of modern science the church always taught that the gift of tongues was the power to speak in one or more historical languages: e.g., Greek, French, or Chinese. Modern liberals introduced the theory that it was an incomprehensible babble. And in this, they are generally supported by the modern "tongues" propagandists. Whether a man has actually the power to speak in Greek, German, or Japanese is a simple matter of fact and not a proper subject for religious controversy. If he has it, and never learned it from man, then he has a divine gift, quite equal to the power to raise the dead. If few have it, we dare not find any fault with the Holy Spirt, who "giveth to every man severally as he will."

Preachers and Elders

However, examination of these gifts discloses that only one of them is of a nature to demand all of a man's time for its operation. That is the gift of prophecy, which means preaching or teaching. This is a gift which Paul says is more profitable than that of tongues; it is a gift very abundant in the church in all ages. When the churches sought to find a place for the man with the prophetic calling, it dared not equate his work with that of the priest; for heathen priests were regarded as archenemies of God because they served the gods of idolatry, which were regarded as demons by both Christians and Jews. Jewish priests could not serve in the new dispensation. Moreover, all Christians were declared priests in the new Israel which was the church.

Fortunately there was in the Jewish religion an office with suggestive possibilities—the elder in the synagogue. Throughout all the Jewish Dispersion the elder, although not primarily a preacher, was a very distinguished person. Everywhere the Jews were allowed by the Roman Empire to manage their local communities in their own way. Therefore, in their local synagogues they not only held schools for the teaching of the young, they also held courts for the administration of local affairs. Twice a week these courts were held, and the elders sat as judges. They could sentence a man to be beaten with thirty-nine stripes, they could fine him, or they could even excommunicate him from the Jewish community, in which case his condition would be tragic indeed. It was to this office that the Christians assigned the new order of prophets who were rising among them. "They ordained them elders in every church."

There is also evidence that these Jewish elders with their

gifts of administration and government were frequently transferred to the eldership in the church when a larger number
of Jews left the synagogue and went into the church. This
gave rise temporarily to what seemed like two kinds of elders
in the early church. "Let the elders that rule well be counted
worthy of double honor [double pay, perhaps], especially they
who labor in the word and doctrine" (I Tim. 5:17). Here the
Apostle refers to the difference between the older type of
Jewish elders—men of social prestige and administrative
talent—and the new type of youthful Christian elders—prophetic men with aptitude for teaching and social contacts. The
prophet was the man called of God; the elder was a prophetic
man recognized in office by the church. Sometimes the church
neglects its duty and the prophet is never recognized as an
elder.

The Order of Deacons

By the time a man endures the drudgery necessary to become a New Testament scholar, it is almost impossible for him
to appreciate the informality and spontaneity of that great
book. The New Testament is a song of victory, and the
scholars have been forced to draw all their philosophy and
legal lore from that happy, unself-conscious volume. Take
deacons for example. In the Greek the term simply means a
servant, perhaps a table waiter, and for ages ecclesiastics have
been ordaining deacons as a special kind of "servant," whereas no man can prove that any kind of servant of the church
is not a deacon. Janitors, Sunday school teachers, secretaries,
young people's leaders, church treasurers, trustees, and so
on—all these are deacons. The Seven whose choice is recorded
in Acts 6 are commonly called deacons, although not in the
Bible itself. In I Timothy instructions are given regarding
deacons, but no definition of their work is given. They are
simply servants of the church. For a long time in the ancient
church their number was restricted to seven in each congregation. Finally, the number was doubled, but it always was

restricted. They were the assistants of the bishop in the administration of the church's funds. Because of their limited number as against the vast numbers of the clergy, they often held a superior place.

Among Methodists a deacon is in an inferior order of the ministry; his next step is to be ordained an elder. Many Protestant churches consider the deacons as lay assistants to the pastor. Sometimes they are ordained for life; again, they are elected for a term on a board of deacons. This is better than a life-tenure office, which may embarrass a term-tenure pastor.

THE ORDINANCES OF THE CHURCH

Except for a very small minority the universal Christian church of all sects and parties practices two rites: water baptism and the Lord's Supper. To these a small minority add foot washing. The ritualistic churches call these rites sacraments. We prefer—with many free-church theologians—the term ordinances.

Baptism: *Its Origin and Mode*

The Mosaic law demanded many ceremonial baths and washings as part of the ritual cleansing from uncleanness for any cause. Since Gentiles practiced so many customs regarded as extremely ritualistically unclean, the rabbis demanded from a time before the days of Christ that every male convert from heathenism should not only be circumcised but also undergo a complete immersion as a ritualistic cleansing from his heathen defilement. The striking thing about John's baptism was that he required the people of Israel to repent and be immersed in the same radical manner as if they had been Gentiles. During Christ's earthly ministry his disciples baptized the people on his behalf (John 4:2). After Christ's resurrection, before he ascended into heaven, he commanded his disciples: "Go ye therefore, and teach all nations, baptizing them in the name of the Father, and of the Son, and of the Holy Ghost" (Matt. 28:19).

There is scarcely any point of theological teaching more commonly agreed upon among theological scholars than that the apostolic church at first practiced immersion only; and that other forms such as sprinkling and pouring came in later. Even John Calvin, who after Zwingli may be regarded as the founder of the Reformed and Presbyterian church systems, wrote in his *Institutes*: "The very word baptize, however, signifies to immerse; and it is certain that immersion was the practice of the ancient church." The evidence for immersion is so extensive that space forbids its use here. See my *The Apostolic Church* (pp. 172-204). When Philip baptized the eunuch, "They went down both into the water," and they came "up out of the water" (Acts 8:38). When Jesus was baptized, he "went up straightway out of the water" (Matt. 3:16). Mark speaks of him as ". . . coming up out of the water" (1:10). John the Baptist baptized in Enon "because there was much water there" (John 3:23). Sprinkling would not have required much water.

How did pouring and sprinkling come in? Dr. Henry K. Rowe, Professor of History in the Andover-Newton Theological School, in his *History of the Christian People*, a textbook published in 1931, says:

> The original mode of baptism was by immersion, but after a time it became modified to pouring or sprinkling water upon those who were sick, a practice called clinical baptism, and the practice was extended to others. Yet until late in the Middle Ages the form of immersion was the official form in the West and has remained customary in the East.

Briefly, this is what happened: The early church taught living above sin. But as the spiritual tension lessened with the passage of time, multitudes of people hesitated to be immersed for fear they might not be able to live sinless lives. In this way they procrastinated immersion until they came to their deathbed, as did Constantine, the first Christian emperor. On their deathbed many Christians were physically incapable of undergoing immersion. But by this time magical ideas of the power of the water to cleanse had grown and spread, so that it was believed that only a few drops of this holy water would cleanse from sin. In this way affusion—sprinkling or pouring —was substituted for immersion.

Moreover new customs grew up. For instance, in the ancient church the candidates for baptism were called *catechumen*; and were trained in classes for considerable periods. Previous to their baptism, these pupils were dismissed from the services before the Lord's Supper was served to the church. From this dismissal (*dismissus,* in Latin) the Supper gradually came to be called the mass. Owing to its abhorrence of apostasy, the church refused to forgive apostates who fell away under persecution. In course of time, however, mercy prevailed, and the custom arose of sending the apostates back into a line of penitents literally standing outside the church door, very much as the ancient catechumen had stood. After a penitent apostate had stood in a line of penitents like this for a period of time varying from three months to many years, he was finally pardoned and taken back into the church. This discipline was all administered by the whole church at first; but in time, it was taken over by the priests, and became the origin of the sacrament of penance and absolution, by which the priest forgave every sin and admitted any sinner back into church fellowship.

After the rise of this custom, there was no longer the necessity of living above sin after baptism. The Christian who fell into sin could be neatly and easily cleansed and restored without public reproach or humiliation. From this time baptism was turned back to infancy, and most Christians were baptized as babes. In the Oriental churches infants were and are immersed down to the present time. In the Roman church, and later in most Protestant churches, the sprinkling or pouring of the ancient deathbed baptism is continued into the modern age.

The Symbolism of Baptism

The first figurative meaning of baptism was that the convert had been cleansed from his past sins. Owing to the ever hovering magic and superstition the idea soon took hold that the water itself literally washed away sin; and the words of Scripture have been tortured to teach that theory. In fact some modern scholars have gone so far as to assert that ancient thought was incapable of grasping the idea of spiritual cleansing. Fortunately we have proof that this theory is false. The great Jewish historian Josephus (who lived in the times of Christ, A.D. 37-95) wrote:

> And so to come to baptism; for that washing would be acceptable to him, if they made use of it, not in order to the putting away of some sins, but for the purification of the body; supposing still that the soul was thoroughly purified beforehand by righteousness.[9]

Moreover we have positive proof from the Bible itself that the ceremonial washings of the Mosaic law were merely symbols of cleansing and not magically self-operating. In the ceremony of cleansing the leper, described in Leviticus 14:3, the point is made very clear that the ceremonial cleansing of leprosy was by no means to be used until the leper was in himself actually healed.

Baptism is a symbol of burial. To the symbolism of cleansing, long attached to ceremonial immersion in Israel (note the cleansing of Naaman), the New Testament added the idea that the convert, having been made one with Christ, has died with Christ at his crucifixion and been raised with him in his resurrection. And this Paul teaches in Romans 6. The convert is buried with Christ "by baptism into death: that like as Christ was raised up from the dead by the glory of the Father, even so we also should walk in newness of life" (vs. 4). Not only is baptism a figure of the spiritual resurrection; it is also a symbol of the final resurrection of the dead, when we enjoy the "adoption, to wit, the redemption of our body" (8:23). Again Paul writes: "Buried with him in baptism" (Col. 2:12).

---

[9]In *Antiquities of the Jews*, Book 18, chap. 5, sec. 2.

The Formula of Baptism

Undoubtedly Christ commanded that baptism should be in the name of the triune God—the Father, Son, and Holy Ghost (Matt. 28:19). But in our time there has revived one of the most ancient heresies (Sabellianism), and these "Jesus Only" people refuse to use the name of the Father and of the Holy Spirit in the baptismal formula, claiming that in the Book of Acts people were said to be baptized in the name of Jesus only. It is true that in the Acts people are sometimes described as being baptized in the name of Jesus, but this is not meant to define the formula, but rather the purpose of their baptism.

The name of anything was regarded as very important in ancient thought. Paul says that the hosts of Israel were all baptized unto Moses when they passed through the cloud and the sea (I Cor. 10:2). He does not mean to say that someone stood over them and pronounced Moses' name. The intent of their baptism was to commit them publicly to Moses' discipleship, and this discipleship they followed till a greater than Moses came. Then they were baptized unto Christ to be his disciples.

Fortunately we have proof that to be baptized in the name of the Trinity is in fact baptism in the name of Christ. In the *Didache,* an ancient Christian document dated about A.D. 150 (?) we read: "And concerning baptism, thus baptize ye: Having first said all these things, baptize into the name of the Father, and of the Son, and of the Holy Spirit, in living water" (chap. 7). Yet in chapter 9:5 of the same book we read in directions concerning the Lord's Supper: "But let no one eat or drink of your Thanksgiving (Eucharist), but they who have been baptized into the name of the Lord." Here one of the oldest Christian documents outside the New Testament says that a person who has been baptized in the name of the Father and of the Son and of the Holy Ghost has in fact been baptized, as the Book of Acts says, in the name of the Lord Jesus.

Baptism Not for Infants

Not once in the New Testament is there a clear instance of the baptism of infants. Everywhere in the New Testament faith precedes conversion, and conversion goes before baptism. "Repent and be baptized," is the scriptural order. Again there is not space for the evidence. See my *Apostolic Church*. Dr. J. L. Neve in his *History of Christian Thought*, writes: "During the first centuries adult baptism was practiced." Dr. Adolf Deissman speaks of the ancient Christians as having been "baptized as adults." J. Neander says, "We have no testimony regarding it [infant baptism] from earlier times," i.e., before the second century.

We find the strange idea persisting down to the present time that baptism replaces circumcision in the Christian dispensation. Here are evidences to the contrary: (1) Before the time of Christ Jewish converts from heathenism were both circumcised and baptized. (2) At the Council of Jerusalem (Acts 15) it was tacitly agreed that Jewish Christians would continue to be both circumcised and baptized. This shows that one rite had not replaced the other. (3) Paul circumcised Timothy whose mother was a Jewess (16:3). Therefore he made a clear distinction between the two rites, as Timothy had already been baptized as a Christian. (4) Furthermore, if circumcision was the rite of admission to the immutable covenant of God, then it follows that those who had been circumcised would need no other admission. No circumcised Jew in Christ's time would ever have been baptized and thus nullify God's ancient covenant. (5) If baptism is the ceremonial equivalent of circumcision, then it is an evil thing in our present stage of advancement; for Paul says, "Behold, I Paul say unto you, that if ye be circumcised, Christ shall profit you nothing" (Gal. 5:2). Then if baptism is equivalent to circumcision (which we deny) it is profitless.

At bottom the theory of infant baptism grows out of the false belief that infants are guilty of something for which they need to be forgiven; and that there is magic power in the water to wash away this stain of sin.

The real danger in infant baptism is one which multitudes of intelligent people are seeing today. It robs millions of professed Christians of any personal commitment to Christ. All over the world are vast multitudes of people who can never know the thrill of personal commitment and conversion because they believe their parents have already done this all-important work for them. This lack of personal experience with Christ is the very death stroke for Christianity in myriads of homes. It is as if children were married in their infancy, and went into adult life robbed of all the thrill of courtship and marriage.

The Lord's Supper

On the night before his death our Lord "took bread, and blessed it, and brake it, and gave it to the disciples, and said, Take, eat; this is my body. And he took the cup, and gave thanks, and gave it to them, saying, Drink ye all of it; for this is my blood of the new testament, which is shed for many for the remission of sins" (Matt. 26:26-28). See Mark 14:22-24; Luke 22:19-20; I Corinthians 11:23-30. The sacerdotal churches—that is, those professing to have a priesthood (Roman Catholic, Eastern Orthodox, Anglican, and others)—hold that this bread and wine constitute the real body and blood of Christ when they have been properly blessed by the priest. Most Protestant and all evangelical churches believe that the bread and wine become symbols of the body and blood of Christ.

In the early ages of the church the Lord's Supper was celebrated at the end of the feast of charity—a free feast provided for the poor Christians by the love of the congregation, quite like the old-fashioned basket dinners of early American days. This food was brought as offerings by the congregation, and when the meal began the presiding minister prayed a prayer of dedication, offering the whole as a gift to the Lord. In the

passage of ages, the people began to consider the church too
holy to eat the feast of charity in; therefore they took it to
their own homes, and continued the Supper only in the church.
Then when the minister prayed the prayer of dedication, he
finally came to think that he was offering the body and blood
of Christ as a repetition of the sacrifice of Christ on the cross.

This was the origin of the theory that the Lord's Supper is
a sacrifice. In ancient times, this sacrifice of the Mass was
offered on the tombs of martyrs who had died for Christ. When
the church forbade this, the bones of the martyrs were brought
from the tombs and enshrined in the altars in the church.
Therefore to this day, no Roman priest can say Mass at any
altar not containing the bones of some saint.

When the Lord ate the Last Supper with his disciples it was
during a yearly feast, and this might suggest an annual observance. However, no set time is given for its observance.
The Apostle merely said: "As often as ye eat this bread, and
drink this cup, ye do show the Lord's death till he come"
(I Cor. 11:26). Some churches teach that it must be observed
every Sunday, following what they claim is the example of the
church as recorded in Acts 2:42, 46. First, we notice that the
partaking of food noted here was a feature of the great revival
and its rich fellowship wherein all the people ate freely of
the abounding charity of the congregation. If we are bound to
follow this literally, then we must have the Supper, not only
on Sunday, but on every day, along with other food provided
by the charity of the church.

Foot Washing

"And supper being ended . . . he . . . began to wash the disciples' feet, and to wipe them with the towel wherewith he was
girded" (John 13:2-5). Many Christians have recognized that
Jesus here instituted a third ordinance of the church to be
observed along with immersion and the Supper. Foot washing
was observed in the ancient church to the days of Augustine,
and beyond. In his *Replies to Questions of Januarius* (Book

II, chap. 18, sec. 33), Augustine, the great Latin Father, says that in his day foot washing was practiced by some of the Christians of his diocese. It was practiced all over Europe in the early ages; and although the Council of Elvira forbade it about A.D. 306, the Synod of Toledo (A.D. 694) excluded from the Communion table those who refused to take part in foot washing on Maunday Thursday, the Thursday before Easter.

The rite of foot washing teaches humility and the spirit of forgiveness. It is the little baptism, as Jesus intimated; for while it is possible to live without offending God and having to repeat the baptism for the forgiveness of sins, it is not possible—on account of our human limitations and feebleness—to live without sometimes unintentionally offending a brother. Therefore we wash each other's feet, as a symbol of our continuous forgiveness of our brothers. Foot washing also teaches service in the lowliest ways. It honors Christ in the waiters and servants, in the scrubwomen, in the men who dig ditches and plow fields, in all that vast army who carry on the dirty and wearisome work of the world.

Who Should Administer the Ordinances?

There are those who think that the administration of the Supper and of baptism is restricted to a certain order of the priesthood. The New Testament teaches that all Christians are priests. It is never possible for one Christian to be more of a priest than another; for only Christ is our great High Priest. Doubtless all Christians have something of the grace and the spirit of prophecy. But some Christians are so clearly endowed with the gift of prophecy that they are called to devote all their time to the ministry. It is our duty to honor their ministry; therefore, as a courtesy they doubtless should be preferred in the administration of the ordinances. But in case of need, any Christian as one of the priesthood of believers may proceed with the administration of any of the ordinances of the Lord's house. "Only let all things be done decently and in order" (I Cor. 14:40).

PART THREE

THE WORK OF CHRIST AS KING

Chapter IX

CHRIST AS LORD OF LIFE

The doctrine of the kingship of Christ covers such subjects as Christ's lordship of the moral life of the Christian, both private and public; Christ's lordship of his church; Christ's kingdom and reign; and Christ's second coming.

CHRISTIAN ETHICS

The Highest Good

From the days of the great Greek thinkers, the goal of life has been conceived in terms of the highest good—called in Christian literature for a thousand years and more the *summum bonum* (Latin for "the highest good"). Setting the goal in such terms has engendered no little controversy. In our time, perhaps the best-known purpose of life is to be happy. It is generally assumed among Christians that the Christian way of life will best conduce to one's happiness. Regarded thus, the goal has its value, but it has also a serious weakness, inasmuch as it makes self the object of life's purpose. Another directive is similar: "Live so as to give your better self its most complete expression." This idea likewise has value, but carries the same fault as the first. Still another motto, "Live according to reason" is like planning a trip to Europe on five dollars. First there is not enough of one kind of resource; second, more kinds are needed.

Here we turn to the Christian tradition for light. The West-minster Shorter Catechism (1647) says "Question 1: What is the chief end of man? Answer. Man's chief end is to glorify God, and to enjoy him forever." This is similar to the New Testament text: "No man can say that Jesus is the Lord, but by the Holy Ghost" (I Cor. 12:3).

The highest good of the Christian life cannot be better ex-pressed than by the use of the most hated word in the modern world—slavery. Man belongs to God, and his highest good is found when he returns to the divine ownership. In fact (as elsewhere explained) the primary meaning of holiness is di-vine ownership and the moral character such ownership in-volves. In thinking of service to Christ as slavery one must purge his mind of all the evil associations of the word. We belong to God, just as we belong to our mothers and our families, to our nation, to our tribe, and to our friends; just as we belong to the hills where we (perhaps) played as chil-dren, and from which we can never depart, though we flee to the uttermost parts of the earth. Love can purge slavery of degradation and change it to pride.

Choosing a Vocation

The word vocation means "calling," and it is the duty of a Christian to submit his heart to the call of God for life's ser-vice. The Christian ministry is far from being the only calling for a Christian man. Undoubtedly there are conditions of life and society in which a Christian man can actually build up the Kingdom better outside than inside the ministry. No one knows this of you better than the Holy Spirit who gives you your life vocation. Doubtless the greatest mistake in choosing a calling is simply to set out to make a living. The Christian's duty is to make a life. In some cases he can be at his best toil-ing in a trade. In ancient Israel every man was taught a trade. And the plan has moral value.

In the old days many parents urged their children to get an education in order to avoid hard work. This was always poor advice. Other things being equal, a man is likely to get the most enjoyment and benefit out of the hardest work he can do either physically or mentally. But with the advance of machinery, the danger is that a man will neglect his education because it is easier to tend an automatic machine at high wages than to develop his mind through the labor and sacrifice necessary to get an education.

The Use of Leisure

Our machine age has an ethical problem of an exceptional nature. Many young people suffer complete moral disintegration because they do not know how to occupy their excessive leisure time. Most teachers find it hard to sympathize with this difficulty, as usually the teacher is a person who has been driven by his tasks from childhood. Doubtless there is a place for body-building sports and healthful recreation. But undoubtedly there are many Christian youth among us with sufficient intelligence to utilize their leisure fruitfully in the development of hobbies of a useful nature like making furniture and other utilities around a modern home. Then come music, painting, learning languages (phonograph courses make this method perfect), cultural reading, and the like. Educated young people might well devote some time to learning how to write juvenile literature and even fiction for adults. In addition, one can mention a reasonable amount of time given to Bible reading and private devotion. The writer has read the Old Testament through eighteen times and the New Testament forty-five times.

Certainly no minister need worry about too much leisure. If he is a college and seminary graduate he can go on and become a scholar in Bible studies, by reading the Bible continuously in Hebrew and Greek and keeping up with theological research. In addition to all this, the Christian can employ a great deal of leisure in definite Christian work and in attendance at the services of the congregation.

Bear gravely in mind that these fruitful uses of leisure are important in the building of a personality and a life which must be examined before the eternal Judge. For if men must give account for every idle word, how much more so for every idle hour and every idle work which was not fruitful for the needs of human life.

Our generation has been trained in the idea that enjoyment is the purpose of life. We need a fresh realization of the sacredness of work. Man works to express his personality. The form which his labor puts upon physical objects is an expression of the gift of creatorship which the Lord bestowed upon him when he made him a man with the eye and the hand of an artist. The deepest of all satisfactions, aside from spiritual ecstasy, is the pleasure derived from honest work in which a man not only lays a creative hand upon the unfinished earth, but also contributes mightily to his own character and personality development.

The Developing Christian Life

We reject the idea that a Christian ever attains maturity in this life. Maturity means the end of growth, and the Christian must grow in grace throughout life. The Christian life is the life of faith pre-eminently, and as such its enduring, indispensable condition is insecurity and alertness. The sense of mystery and the growing awareness of one's ignorance are the rewards of growth in grace and in the knowledge of the truth. This makes the Christian life as fresh and as challenging as it ever was, until the soul has penetrated life's last mystery. The Scriptures teach a Christian perfection when the work of redemption is completed. But this is not maturity; it is only the proper condition for growth in grace. As long as we are on probation we can never become mature or secure, in the sense that we no longer need faith.

MARRIAGE AND DIVORCE

The norm of Christian marriage is the union of one man and one woman for life. "For this cause shall a man leave father and mother, and shall cleave to his wife: and they twain shall be one flesh. Wherefore they are no more twain, but one flesh. What therefore God hath joined together, let no man put asunder" (Matt. 19:5). Being one flesh means that they are not only joined spiritually but in the flesh. Therefore their marriage can never be ideally dissolved till the flesh of one is dead. This is certainly the Christian ideal of marriage.

Nevertheless, Christ himself asserted that marriage could be killed by the infidelity of either partner. We say, "either partner," although Christ mentioned only the sin of the wife as justifying divorce. Nevertheless, on the principle of Paul, that in Christ "there is neither male nor female" (Gal. 3:28), we are bound to apply this restriction to both sexes. Chastity is not merely a female virtue. The passage in question reads, "And I say unto you, Whosoever shall put away his wife, except it be for fornication, and shall marry another, committeth adultery: and whosoever marrieth her which is put away doth commit adultery" (Matt. 19:9). The Roman Catholic Church disallows this inferred permission to the innocent party to remarry in case of a marriage broken by adultery, but most Protestant churches permit the innocent party to marry again. We need not fear following Christ's teaching here. Nevertheless, the accusation of infidelity is easily made and hard to prove; so that the conscience of the parties involved is always an important factor.

Every Christian ought to remember that any scriptural grounds of divorce are to be regarded, like the instruments of the surgeon, as things which might help cure a dreaded tragedy in one's life, but by no means to be contemplated as means to a normal existence. The best psychologists teach that any marriage can endure if both parties are willing. This fact must put a burden of guilt upon the unwilling partner which no bright skies nor wealthy surroundings can relieve. Yet we must acknowledge that a marriage that has been killed by one partner cannot be revived by the other acting alone. Moreover we have no warrant in Scripture to ask a person to withdraw from an unscriptural marriage and return to a former companion. Let the dead bury their dead.

WOMEN IN THE CHURCH

It is a simple historical fact that heathenism and Islam have contributed to the degradation of woman. Judaism and Christianity, on the contrary, have exalted her. It must be admitted, however, that both Judaism and Christianity exalted womanhood most in their seasons of spiritual revival. Thus Miriam the prophetess exercised her prophetic office in the great moment of spiritual fervor when Israel gloried in her deliverance after passing through the Red Sea (Exod. 15:20). Deborah became a prophetess in a crisis of history (Judg. 4:4). Then, when the first coming of the Son of God began to send a radioactive thrill as it were through the world of that time, Anna the prophetess appeared in the Temple to welcome the infant Christ (Luke 2:36). And so we find prophetesses in the church at Corinth and in the family of Philip. Prophetesses appeared among the Anabaptists and in the great Wesleyan revival.

Women preached in the New Testament church. Proof of this is that preaching and prophesying are the same. "He that prophesieth speaketh unto men to edification, and exhortation, and comfort" (I Cor. 14:3), and that is preaching. Now women preached at Corinth, for the Apostle told them how to dress when preaching (11:5). True, he commanded the woman to wear a veil while preaching, but that was only in conformity to a custom of the country that counted it a mark of immorality for an unveiled woman to appear in public. It is true that Paul commanded women to be silent in the church, but it is evident this injunction was intended to curb the disorders of ignorant heathen women, for in the same book he gave orders as to the dress and behavior of a Christian woman preacher. Moreover the four daughters of Philip were all preachers in the apostolic age (Acts 21:9).

CHRIST IS LORD OF THE SABBATH

Every Bible student knows that many ceremonies were embedded in the Mosaic legislation, which were merely typical of the spiritual blessing of the new covenant and which were therefore done away with at the coming of Christ. These blessings stand in the New Testament as the spiritual antitypes of the ancient ritual. Some of these ceremonies are admitted as typical by all Christians. Take, for example, the sacrifices of the Old Testament which were types of Christ as priest, as altar, and as victim. The tabernacle and temple shadow forth the plan of salvation and of the church. Circumcision is a type of entire sanctification (not of baptism).

Old Testament Sabbath a Type

While not all agree that the Sabbath is also such a type, the New Testament does so teach. The Book of Hebrews is devoted to an exposition of the types of the Old Testament. The latter part of the third and first part of the fourth chapters of that book contain such an exposition of the Sabbath, teaching that the Sabbath of the Old Testament was a type of the spiritual rest which remains for the people of God. Notice in reading this passage that the Greek word for the Joshua of the Old Testament is Jesus, which is also the name of the Savior.

Here the writer likens the rest of the soul found in Christ to the rest of the Old Testament Sabbath (4:7). God rested from the work of creation after having worked through six ages of time. That the days of creation were ages is proved by the fact that the rest day of God which followed creation was likewise an age which is not yet ended. Now when man imitates the rest of God physically he rests for only a twenty-four-hour day (the Mosaic Sabbath). But when at last man was admitted into the true spiritual rest, that proved to be an eternal rest of the soul which reaches into eternity. This is the rest which the Jewish Sabbath typified. It is a rest which we find in Christ.

The Sabbath and the Ten Commandments

Many people regard the Sabbath as binding throughout all time because it is embedded in the Ten Commandments which could not be rescinded without breaking down the moral order of the world. The Sabbath commandment is the only ceremonial or ritual commandment among the Ten. Now we find every one of the moral commandments repeated in the New Testament—but not the Sabbath Commandment. Notice again that legal codes can change without changing moral principles.

Once I lived in Detroit. There had been in order there Indian tribal government, French Colonial, British Colonial, American Territorial, and Michigan State governmental codes. Each in turn condemned murder. A man who murders in Michigan today does not violate Indian, French, British, or American Territorial law, for these are all passed away. Such a criminal however violates Michigan State law. When a man commits murder today, he does not violate the Ten Commandments (we might say), but he violates the New Testament which brands murder as sin.

The Ten Commandments Rescinded

Remembering that every moral principle in the Ten Commandments is repeated and reaffirmed in the New Testament, we shall prove that the Sabbath of the Old Testament is rescinded, because the Ten Commandments as a code of law is done away with the rest of Old Testament legislation. The Ten Commandments are the old covenant.

1. A new covenant was promised: "Behold, the days come, saith the Lord, that I will make a new covenant with the house of Israel, and with the house of Judah" (Jer. 31:31).

2. The Mosaic covenant was temporary: "He is the mediator of a better covenant, which was established upon better promises" (Heb. 8:6).

3. The Ten Commandments were that old covenant: "And he [Moses] wrote upon the tables the words of the covenant,

the Ten Commandments" (Exod. 34:28). "And he declared unto you his covenant . . . even Ten Commandments; and he wrote them upon two tables of stone" (Deut. 4:13). "The Lord our God made a covenant with us in Horeb . . . [then follow the Ten Commandments] and he added no more. And he wrote them in two tables of stone" (5:2-22). "When I was gone up into the mount to receive the tables of stone, even the tables of the covenant . . . the Lord gave me the two tables of stone, even the tables of the covenant" (9:9-11). These tables of stone were in the ark in the days of Solomon. "And I have set there a place for the ark, wherein is the covenant of the Lord, which he made with our fathers" (I Kings 8:21). "But there was nothing in the ark save the two tables of stone which Moses put there at Horeb, when the Lord made a covenant with the children of Israel" (vs. 9). The writer of Hebrews knew that the Ten Commandments were the tables of the covenant. ". . . and the ark of the covenant . . . wherein was the golden pot . . . and the tables of the covenant" (9:4). This is the covenant which was done away.

4. The Law was given for a limited time and purpose: "For the law was our schoolmaster to bring us unto Christ, that we might be justified by faith" (Gal. 3:24).

5. The Law is restated in the gospel: "For the priesthood being changed, there is made of necessity a change also of the law" (Heb. 7:12).

6. Therefore the Sabbath of the Old Testament is done away. "Know ye not, brethren, . . . the woman which hath an husband is bound. . . . But if her husband be dead, she is free from that law. . . . Ye also are become dead to the law by the body of Christ" (Rom. 7:1-4).

"Forasmuch as ye are manifestly declared to be the epistle of Christ ministered by us, written not with ink, but with the Spirit of the living God; not in tables of stone, but in fleshly tables of the heart. . . . But if the ministration of death, written and engraven in stones, was glorious . . . which glory was to be done away: how shall not the ministration of the spirit be rather glorious?" (II Cor. 3:3-8). "These are the two covenants; the one from the mount Sinai, which gendereth to bondage, which is Agar. . . . But Jerusalem which is above is free, which is the mother of us all" (Gal. 4:24-26). The writer of Hebrews knows a "better covenant" (8:6). "In that he saith, A new covenant, he hath made the first old. Now that which decayeth and waxeth old is ready to vanish away" (vs. 13). Christ is "the mediator of the new covenant" (12:24). Paul says that Christ has blotted out the handwriting of ordinances, and adds, "Let no man therefore judge you . . . in respect of . . . the sabbath days" (Col. 2:14-16).

The Old Testament Sabbath was, of course, observed on the seventh day of the week, or Saturday (Exod. 20:8-10). The custom of Sunday observance rests upon the practice of the apostolic church. "And they rose up the same hour, and returned to Jerusalem, and found the eleven gathered together, and them that were with them" (Luke 24:33). "Then the same day at evening, being the first day of the week, when the doors were shut where the disciples were assembled for fear of the Jews, came Jesus and stood in the midst, and saith unto them, Peace be unto you. . . . And after eight days again his disciples were within, and Thomas with them: then came Jesus, the doors being shut, and stood in the midst, and said, Peace be unto you" (John 20:19, 26). "And when the day of Pentecost was fully come, they were all with one accord in one place" (Acts 2:1). "And we sailed away from Philippi after the days of unleavened bread, and came unto them to Troas in five days; where we abode seven days. And upon the first day of the week when the disciples came together to break bread, Paul preached unto them, ready to depart on the morrow; and continued his speech until midnight" (20:6-7). "Now concerning the collection for the saints, as I have given order to the churches of Galatia, even so do ye. Upon the first day of the week let every one of you lay by him in store, as God hath prospered him (I Cor. 16:1-2).

Chapter X

CHRIST REIGNS IN HIS KINGDOM

The Kingdom of God and the Church

As the doctrine of the kingdom of God—or of heaven, for they are synonymous—develops in the Bible, it is presented under so many forms and in so many aspects that it requires diligence to grasp it. Perhaps the easiest way to distinguish between the church and the kingdom is to think of the church as an institution (remembering many reservations) and the kingdom as the dynamic that runs the church. The kingdom of God is like the inner physiological processes that make the human body function (the beat of the heart, the reaction of the nerves, the thrill of human life), whereas the church is that body of Christ functioning objectively in the world of mankind. Again, the kingdom of God has many phases. God is King of all nature; he rules in the kingdoms of men, over the nations. On the head of Christ are many crowns. Undoubtedly some phases of his kingdom were at work in ancient Israel, and even in the world of mankind from the beginning.

The Kingdom Is Spiritual

The Kingdom parables give us a view of the richness and variety of the conceptions which enter into the kingdom of God.

However, in the sense emphasized in the New Testament, the kingdom of God is the moral realm and the spiritual power of Christ in his work as Messiah and Mediator. This power moves out from Christ like magnetism. It touches and motivates people not yet come into the historic fellowship of the church. Thus Christ said that the understanding scribe was "not far from the kingdom of God" (Mark 12:34).

The spiritual and incorporeal nature of the Kingdom is indicated by the fact that "the kingdom of God is not in word, but in power" (I Cor. 4:20). "The kingdom of God is not meat and drink; but righteousness, and peace, and joy in the Holy Ghost" (Rom. 14:17). It is not visible, like the church: "The kingdom of God cometh not with observation: neither shall they say, Lo here! or, lo there! for, behold, the kingdom of God is within you" (Luke 17:20-21). It is true that the Revised Standard Version says "among," but the American Standard Version, Williams, and Goodspeed say "within." Some good scholars who write it "among" do not deny its spiritual, intangible nature. They say, "It was not 'within' the hardened Pharisees, but among them in invisible form, the Spirit of Christ himself."

Thus the kingdom is broader than the church. It is that invisible, intangible power that worketh for righteousness in all mankind. It is an effect of the shining of that Light that lighteth every man. It is the power that saves beyond the reach of the church. On the other hand, the church is the body of Christ, the fellowship of the consciously redeemed by the historic ministry of the Word of God. In some scriptural accounts the church and the kingdom almost completely merge and are practically identical, but when a distinction is seen, the kingdom is broader than the church and functions beyond its historic borders. By no means should we limit the kingdom of God to the fringes of his influence.

Christ Is King Forever

Christ is King of the kingdom of God in the sense that the gospel rests on the basis of his death, and his kingship consists of his exercise of his mediatorial function as Savior to sinners. He is King of the church as much or more than elsewhere. This is the kingdom of grace, the interior life of religion. In a sense this is what men mean by the term, "the church invisible," because, as a matter of course, the mediatorial reign of Christ includes all the saved in heaven and earth.

"Then cometh the end, when he shall have delivered up the kingdom to God, even the Father; when he shall have put down all rule and all authority and power" (I Cor. 15: 24). This means that after the judgment Christ will, as it were, close the books on the whole mediatorial work of salvation. He will resign his mediatorial kingship to the Father. Nevertheless, he will be eternal King as Head of the church; as such, "of his kingdom there shall be no end" (Luke 1: 33). The practical value of this text is to teach us solemnly that the plan of salvation as a process will come to an end.

Death and Immortality

As Christians we do not dare stake the immortality of the soul upon the arguments of philosophy, either of ancient Greece or of modern times. The Bible nowhere tries to prove the immortality of the soul, even as it makes no effort to prove the existence of God. But in the Old Testament there was the persistent belief in life after death for all men, the souls of men continuing to exist in a place called Sheol. This Sheol is called Hades in the New Testament. However, in the New Testament Hades is no longer a place, but a state or condition.

Throughout the New Testament immortality is taken for granted. Not only is heaven filled with legions of angels, but the souls of the blessed are with Christ. He leads them by fountains of living waters and wipes away all tears from their eyes. Paul feels sure that to depart this life is to be with Christ. And he had an experience in which he was not sure whether he was in the body or out of the body. The wicked also live on in eternity. The rich man suffers in hell while the blessed Lazarus finds peace "in the bosom of Abraham," a figure of paradise. At the great judgment the souls of the wicked go away into everlasting punishment, and the righteous into life eternal. Hades is the general state of the dead, good and evil; paradise is the part of Hades inhabited by the saints.

It is in the place called heaven where Jesus is. Gehenna is the part of Hades where the damned suffer in the eternal fire of hell. The Scriptures teach that the works of the dead follow their earthly life. For good and evil there is an accumulation of reward and penalty to be assessed at the judgment and endured or enjoyed in the final hell or heaven which follows the sentence of judgment.

The Second Coming of Christ

When Christ went away to heaven, angels promised his sorrowing disciples: "This same Jesus, which is taken up from you into heaven, shall so come in like manner" (Acts 1:11). "Behold, he cometh with clouds; and every eye shall see him, and they also which pierced him: and all kindreds of the earth shall wail because of him" (Rev. 1:7). This proves that Christ will not come secretly and "steal away" his saints. It also shows that the wicked dead will be raised in time to see this marvel.

"For the Lord himself shall descend from heaven with a shout, with the voice of the archangel, . . . and the dead in Christ shall rise first: then we which are alive and remain shall be caught up" (I Thess. 4:16-17). This does not mean that the dead in Christ will rise before the wicked dead; the saints already dead will rise before the living saints are caught up.

The General Resurrection

"The hour is coming, in which all that are in the graves shall hear his voice, and shall come forth; they that have done good, unto the resurrection of life; and they that have done evil, unto the resurrection of damnation" (John 5:28-29). This shows that the righteous and wicked shall both be raised at the same time. "I charge thee therefore before God, and the Lord Jesus Christ, who shall judge the quick and the dead at his appearing and his kingdom" (II Tim. 4:1). "Because he hath appointed a day, in the which he will judge the world in righteousness by that man whom he hath ordained" (Acts 17:31).

And then there is the description of the judgment in Matthew 25: "When the Son of man shall come in his glory, and all the holy angels with him, then shall he sit upon the throne of his glory: and before him shall be gathered all nations: and he shall separate them one from another, as a shepherd divideth his sheep from the goats. . . . Then shall he say unto them on the left hand, Depart from me, ye cursed, into everlasting fire, prepared for the devil and his angels. . . . And these shall go away into everlasting punishment: but the righteous into life eternal" (vss. 31-46). The righteous are invited, "Come, ye blessed of my Father, inherit the kingdom prepared for you from the foundation of the world" (vs. 34).

Index of Subjects

Index of Scripture References